BUILDING RESILIENCY in *Children*

A Trauma-Informed Activity Guide for Children

Also from the Boys Town Press

Building Resiliency in Youth: A Trauma-Informed Guide for Working with Youth in Schools
Building Resiliency in Teens: A Trauma-Informed Workbook for Teens
Teaching Social Skills to Youth, 3rd Ed.
Teaching Social Skills to Youth with Mental Health Disorders
Well-Managed Schools, 2nd Ed.
Tools for Teaching Social Skills in School
More Tools for Teaching Social Skills in School
Everyone's Talking
Take Two: Skill-Building Skits You Have Time to Do!
13 & Counting: Be the Difference
13 & Counting: Does a Hamburger Really Have to Be Round?
13 & Counting: Rescue Me
GRIT & Bear It!
GRIT & Bear It! Activity Guide
Zest: Live It
Zest: Live It Activity Guide
Effective Study Strategies for Every Classroom
Positive Alternatives to Suspension
School Administrator's Resource Guide
Working with Aggressive Youth
Adolescence and Other Temporary Mental Disorders (DVD)
No Room for Bullies
Safe and Healthy Secondary Schools
Common Sense Parenting®

For Children

Freddie and Friends: Bugging Out
Freddie and Friends: Becoming Unstuck
Opal Octopus is Overwhelmed
My Day is Ruined!
Of Course It's a Big Deal!
Mindset Matters
Stress Stinks

For a free Boys Town Press catalog, call 1-800-282-6657
Visit our website at BoysTownPress.org

Boys Town National Hotline®
1-800-448-3000
A crisis, resource, and referral number for kids and parents

BUILDING RESILIENCY in *Children*

A Trauma-Informed Activity Guide for Children

Kat McGrady, ED.D., LCPC, NCC

Boys Town, Nebraska

Building Resiliency in Children: A Trauma-Informed Activity Guide for Children

Published by Boys Town Press
Boys Town, NE 68010

Copyright © 2021 by Father Flanagan's Boys' Home

ISBN: 978-1-944882-79-2

All rights reserved. Permission is granted for the purchaser of this resource to reproduce pages 3-100 for classroom or for individual or small group counseling only. No other part of this book may be reproduced or transmitted in any form or by any means, electronic or mechanical, including photocopying, recording, or by any information storage and retrieval system, without the written permission of Boys Town Press, except where permitted by law. For information, address Boys Town Press, 13603 Flanagan Blvd., Boys Town, NE 68010 or btpress@boystown.org.

Illustrations by Brian Martin

Graphic design and layout by Anne Hughes

 Boys Town Press is the publishing division of Boys Town, a national organization serving children and families.

10 9 8 7 6 5 4 3 2 1

TABLE OF CONTENTS

Children's Activities: Purpose and Use	1

PROCESSING FEELINGS, EMOTIONS, BEHAVIORS AND ACTIONS

Applesauced	4
Apple Volcano	8
Dancing Seeds	10
What Happens When I Ask for and Accept Help?	12
Worry Worms	14
My Seasons	18
Rotten Apple Pass	25
Control to the Core	26
Candy Apple Coat of Armor	27
Catching the Light	30
Ugly Apple Head	33
Shape Shifting Apple Art	35

COPING, GROUNDING, AND CALMING

Apple Senses	38
Apple Dumpling	40
Sock Worm Buddy	46
Cortland's Warm & Cozy Cider Secret	47
Apple Finger Maze Breathing	50
Grounding Apple Pendulum	52
Progressive Muscle Relaxation (PMR)	54
Worm Wriggle	58
Squeezable Comforting Apple Pie Dough	60
Boosting B.I.N.G.O.	62
Munching Unwelcome Feelings Away	64
Resiliency Travel Kit	66

CONFIDENCE-BOOSTING, STRENGTH, AND RESILIENCE

Chuffle Tree's Challenge	68
Apple POP!	72
One Bad Apple	74
Apple Bird Feeder	76
Superstar Inside	78
Pocket Apple Affirmations	82
Seeds of Gratitude	84
Picking & Choosing Joy	87
Apple Up!	89
The Big Apple	99

CHILDREN'S READ-ALOUD

Children's Read-Aloud Book Prompts	105
Feeling & Frustrations at Sweet Valley Orchard Downloadable Children's Read-Aloud	109

REFERENCES

References	129

Instructions to Download Worksheets and Handouts

ACCESS:

https://www.boystownpress.org/book-downloads

ENTER:

Your first and last names

Email address

Code: 944882BRC792

Check yes to receive emails to ensure your email link is received.

Instructions to Download Children's Read-Aloud and Coloring Pages

ENTER:
(Same as left)

Code: 944882BRCRA792

Children's Activities: Purpose and Use

Children who have been impacted by trauma may benefit significantly from creative and diverse approaches to strengthening resilience and overall well-being. Art, movement, music, sensory, play, and various other experiential approaches that encourage reflection through creative platforms may provide greater opportunities for social, emotional, and cognitive enrichment. The benefits of supporting children and teens through the use of creative approaches are far-reaching.

Use of nonverbal, written expression, and various other creative approaches provides an outlet for children who:

- lack the cognitive ability to fully process and express orally or in writing,
- are developmentally unable to process and express orally or in writing,
- may have hesitations to express orally or in writing, or
- are unable to access implicit memory and the context of thoughts, feelings, or reactions that are stored in implicit memory.

(Hannigan, Grima-Farrell, & Wardman, 2019; Malchiodi, 2012)

Additionally, creative approaches allow children the opportunity to:

- contain trauma or negative material within an object or artform that is safely outside of their own person,
- reduce emotional numbness or other dissociative coping mechanisms,
- feel a sense of connection and belonging by relating abstract or metaphorical self-expression to a more universal theme,
- experience a more equitable platform for self-expression when the ability to hold a fair and balanced conversation with adults and caretakers is unfeasible,
- feel a sense of control over traumatic or negative memories and emotions,
- set their own pace and avoid the anxieties of working under someone else's ideals,

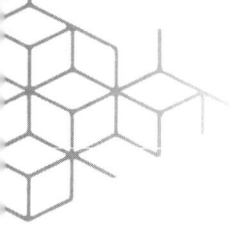

- explore healthy and helpful relaxation strategies in order to reduce hyperarousal or chronic stress,
- feel a sense of empowerment, agency, and accomplishment,
- slowly gain exposure, which increases tolerance and ability to face experiences with confidence and grit,
- enhance problem-solving skills, and/or
- strengthen confidence, self-esteem, and emotional regulation.

(Baker, Metcalf, Varker, & O'Donnell, 2017; Malchiodi, 2012)

This Activity Guide serves to reach children at their developmental, emotional, and cognitive levels using creative and reflective approaches. Each activity is purposeful in targeting the areas of: (a) processing feelings, emotions, behaviors, and actions, (b) coping, grounding, and calming, and (c) confidence-boosting, strength, and resilience. The expressive and creative activities included in this Activity Guide cater to a broad range of individual learning styles, skills, and needs.

Considerations/Food for Thought:

- Allow the child to set the pace and tone.
- Do not force children to complete the activities, to create in a way that meets your expectations, or to be able to discuss their creation upon completion.
- Allow the child to take control, do not give unnecessary directions (although a few directives may be appropriate).
- Do not provide praise during the activity; rather, wait until they have told you they are finished.
- Do not ask leading or probing questions.
- Allow quiet reflective time to occur, let the child lead conversations, and ask open-ended questions.
- Do not make assumptions or pass judgment.
- Remind children that there is no "right or wrong," that these activities are whatever they choose to make them, and that they may take them wherever they would like to take them.

(Malchiodi, 2012; Wait & Ryan, 2019)

Processing Feelings, Emotions, Behaviors, and Actions

Emotional processing involves awareness of emotions, acceptance of and comfort with emotions, and the ability to work through emotions in a healing and nourishing way. Many consider emotional processing to be the first step in strengthening resiliency, as recognizing, understanding, and nonjudgmentally absorbing emotions allows us to choose the best options moving forward.

The following activities are intended to promote healthy emotional processing. They help to build a strong emotional foundation, which then allows for restorative coping and responsiveness as opposed to destructive repression or reaction. These activities are most beneficial when used in the initial stages of a resiliency plan. Emotional processing and reflection should then be a common theme and revisited often thereafter.

BUILDING RESILIENCY IN CHILDREN

Applesauced

Purpose:

Identify and express feelings/emotions.

What you will need:

Set of *Applesauced* cards to cut out and match up

Adult Instructions:

1. Explain that we all feel different emotions sometimes. Share how we sometimes feel:
    - fresh and joyful like a crisp fall apple,
    - warm and calm like apple pie,
    - overall unhappy and mushed like applesauce,
    - scared and in need of protection like a candy apple, or
    - mad like a bitter and tart apple.

2. Brainstorm different words that could describe what it means to feel like a crisp, fresh apple; like apple pie; like applesauce; like a candy apple; and like a bitter, tart apple.

3. Discuss the different emotions that may be felt at different times. Explain how all of these emotions are normal, all of them are okay to have, and that no emotion lasts forever. Explain that emotions come and go like the seasons, even those that are unwelcome.

4. Discuss the importance of recognizing and identifying your emotions. Explain how understanding what we are feeling allows us to better express to others and to get support, better understand our own needs at any given time, and get and give the help needed in order to feel better.

5. Cut out the *Applesauced* cards below. You may use them in the following ways (or get creative and utilize them in another way):

© 2021, Father Flanagan's Boys' Home

VARIATION 1 Emotions Match-Up

Separate the cards into two piles, one pile being the apple emotions, one pile being the description of the physiological symptoms and the experiences. Place the cards face up.

Take turns sharing the body responses or the experiences card, then match each card to the apple emotions card that most likely matches it. Use this to spark discussion about emotions, feelings they cause in your body, how to respond, etc.

VARIATION 2 Share a time when you've felt…

Place the apple emotions cards face down in a pile. Take turns picking a card from the pile, identifying what the emotion could be, and sharing a time when you've felt this way. Use this to spark discussion about emotions, feelings they cause in your body, how to respond, etc.

VARIATION 3 Memory

Place the cards in 4 rows of 3, facing down. Allow the child/children to play Memory by flipping over two cards at a time and trying to match emotion to experience. Use this to spark discussion. Ask questions like, "Why do you feel that these two cards do/do not match?" If it is determined that the two cards match, the child/children may keep them. If not, they must put them back and try to remember their placement for when they flip over the matching cards.

NOTE: There is no wrong answer here. Rather, it is a way to identify and discuss emotions with the child/children and to help them better understand which emotions are evoked in them during times of distress.

**NOTE: Be sure to end the game by revisiting the feelings that align with the apple pie and the fresh crisp apple. Use this time to share out those things that do make the child/children feel warm, safe, happy, excited, etc. Remind them that these people, places, and things are good to think about whenever they are feeling applesauced or any other undesirable emotion.*

Applesauced Card Deck

CARD BACKS

A Trauma-informed Activity Guide for Children

Applesauced Card Deck

CARD FRONTS

Amy Apple was having a rough day. She woke up late, missed breakfast, and forgot her homework. Her best friend noticed that she seemed down and decided to make her a "cheer up" card. This act of kindness made Amy feel like the shiniest apple on earth!

Arlo Apple has a hard time sleeping at night. His tree is too cold, and it has been a harsh season. He has not received the sun and water that he needs to grow strong.

Annie Apple has been having a hard time lately. Her mom and dad are always yelling at each other, and at her. They often say really mean things.

Adam Apple's mom has been diagnosed with apple scab. This apple disease has made her very weak, sick, and unable to be there for him. He does not know if she will recover.

Antwan Apple just moved from another orchard. His new orchard is nothing like his old one. On top of that, his parents are still in the old orchard and he doesn't know when he will see them again.

Ashland Apple just lost her entire orchard community in a woodland fire. She and her family lost everything they owned and now have to start over.

A few of the apples in **Allie Apple's** orchard have been bullying her. They try to make her feel bad and scare her.

WRITE YOUR OWN

WRITE YOUR OWN

WRITE YOUR OWN

WRITE YOUR OWN

WRITE YOUR OWN

NOTE *Front and backs of cards are provided for download and print.*

Apple Volcano

Purpose:

- Demonstrate the need to express feelings/emotions and to express them in healthy ways.
- Illustrate the importance of healthy coping mechanisms.

What you will need:

- 1 apple (more if desired)
- Baking soda
- Vinegar
- 1 paring knife
- 1 spoon
- 1 shallow dish

Adult Instructions:

1. To prepare, use the paring knife to core and scoop out the inside of the apple, making it "bowl-like." It is okay if it is not perfect, as long as you have a semi-hollow inside and a sturdy bottom.

   Save the apple seeds, as you will be using them in the next activity.

2. Reflect on the previous activities.
3. Ask the child/children if they can recall a time when they felt extremely angry, upset, or sad.
4. Ask them what happens when/if they try to hold those feelings in.
5. Ask if they have ever felt that way over and over again.
6. Discuss what it feels like when you bottle emotions up. Discuss/share what happens when you do so consistently over time.
7. Tell the child/children you are going to do an experiment that demonstrates what happens when you bottle your feelings up and try to hold them in.
8. Place the apple in a shallow dish.
9. Tell the child/children that, like the apple seeds in the previous experiment, this apple is filled with feelings. If you'd like, you can ask them to name the apple and describe what it likes to do, where it lives, etc. to give it more personification.

10. Bring out the baking soda. Tell the child/children that the baking soda represents the apple's feeling and emotions. The baking soda represents happy, sad, excited, scared, angry, upset, silly – all of the emotions.

11. Allow the child/children to place a spoonful or two of baking soda inside of the hollowed-out apple.

12. Bring out the vinegar. Tell the child/children that the vinegar is an event or experience that causes unwelcome feelings such as being upset or sad. If you'd like, you can also ask the child/children to describe what this event or experience could be.

13. Ask the child/children what they think will happen when you place one tiny drop of the unwelcome feelings inside of the apple and on its emotions.

14. Have the child/children observe and describe observations as you place one small drop of vinegar inside of the apple.

15. Discuss how some experiences can leave us with unwelcome feelings. Share how the apple is just sitting there, not doing anything to express these emotions or to figure out how to feel better.

16. Ask the child/children what they think will happen if you place another drop of unwelcome feelings inside. Repeat steps 13 and 14.

17. Hand the child/children the vinegar. Ask them what they think will happen if you keep placing the stinky feelings inside of the apple without the apple finding ways to calm themselves and cope.

18. Allow the child/children to pour as much vinegar in as they would like.

19. Discuss what was observed. Ask the child/children how they think this relates to what happens when you leave unwelcome feelings inside without trying to calm or cope.

*NOTE *Add some more fun to this experiment*

If you want to add some more fun to this experiment, bring in a jar of pickled red cabbage! Add the juice from the jar, a little bit at a time, to the baking soda. This makes the foam turn green/bluish. Add vinegar and it turns purple again. You can continue this over and over and use it as a visual indicator to discuss different experiences that could be happening to cause this reaction within the apple.

BUILDING RESILIENCY IN CHILDREN

Dancing Seeds

Purpose:

- Illustrate the importance of identifying and expressing feelings/emotions.
- Demonstrate the importance of getting help and/or allowing supports to provide help.

What you will need:

- Vinegar
- Baking soda
- 1 clear glass
- Leftover apple seeds from the previous experiment, plus more if possible
- 1 spoon

Adult Instructions:

1. Reflect on the previous activity.

2. Tell the child/children that you will be doing an experiment today. Explain that you will be conducting this experiment in order to demonstrate what happens when you allow others to help you, when you identify and express your emotions, and when you find healthy and positive ways to deal with unwelcome feelings and experiences.

3. Ask the child/children to pour the vinegar carefully into the empty clear glass. Allow them to smell it and to think of one word to describe the scent (try to elicit a word like "stinky," "gross," "unpleasant," etc.). Tell them that the vinegar represents experiences that cause unwelcome, or all-around stinky (or whatever other word they chose to describe the smell), feelings.

4. Hand the child/children the apple seeds. Explain that these seeds are like us, filled with emotions and life. If you'd like, you can give them names and personify them a bit more.

5. Ask the child/children what they think will happen when you place the seeds into the glass of experiences that lead to unwelcome (stinky) feelings. Listen and discuss their hypothesis.

6. Allow the child/children to place the seeds in the glass.

7. Note what the child/children observe. Discuss how unwelcome feelings and experiences can sometimes make us feel like we are sinking and can't move. Share a time when you have felt this way *(e.g., if working with a grieving child, share how a close family member's death left you with a sinking, sad, lonely feeling and how you felt like you were stuck)*.

8. Show the child/children the baking soda. Explain the baking soda represents a magic powder. Ask them what they think will happen when you sprinkle this magic powder into the glass and stir. Share thoughts.

9. Have the child/children measure out one small teaspoon of baking powder and ask them to sprinkle it into the glass, then stir.

10. Discuss observations.

11. Explain that identifying emotions and feelings, expressing them, getting help, and finding ways to cope with unwelcome feelings is like the magic powder. These acts will lift you up when you are feeling low and give you the power to dance and feel good again.

12. Ask the child/children to share a time when they have felt like they were sinking and couldn't move. If needed, prompt with another story of when you have felt this way.

13. Ask the child/children to identify what feelings they had. Discuss how labeling feelings helps us to understand what is going on inside of us and helps us to better understand what we can do to feel better.

14. Ask the child/children to share/name three trusted adults (at home, school, etc.) that they could talk to when having unwelcome feelings.

15. If possible, provide the child/children with a prompt and act out how they could express their feelings to trusted adults and how to ask for help (e.g., *"I'm feeling very sad and lonely right now. Could we talk about it?"*).

16. Share a few possible self-soothing/coping strategies that the child/children can easily do on their own. You can refer to the coping strategies section of the guidebook for ideas. If possible, come up with a list of things that make the child/children feel better when they start having unwelcome feelings.

BUILDING RESILIENCY IN CHILDREN

What Happens When I Ask for and Accept Help?

Purpose:

- Understand the importance of asking for and/or receiving help.

What you will need:

- 1 apple
- Lemon juice
- 1 bowl
- 1 knife

Adult Instructions:

1. Reflect on the previous activities.
2. Tell the child/children that you will be conducting an experiment today. Explain that this experiment will help us to better understand what happens when we do not ask for or accept help.
3. Discuss why we sometimes may not want to ask for help or accept it when it is offered (fear, desire to look strong, pride, worried about hurting someone else, confusion, etc.).
4. Cut the apple into halves or quarters.
5. Ask the child/children to pour the lemon juice/squeeze the lemon juice into the bowl.
6. Ask the child/children to place one apple piece into the bowl of lemon juice, making sure that the exposed inside apple flesh is covered in the lemon juice.
7. Explain to the child/children that the lemon juice represents help and support. That it protects the apple and gives it the things it needs to stay healthy and happy.
8. Leave the apple piece in the lemon juice for about 3 minutes, then take out.

9. Place the lemon-soaked apple piece next to the non-soaked apple piece (if you quartered the apples, you may allow the child/children to eat the leftover apple slices).

10. Revisit the apple pieces every 30 minutes or so for up to 2 hours.

11. Share observations. You will notice that the piece soaked in lemon stays bright and light in tint, while the exposed and un-soaked piece gets a darker tint as it is exposed to oxygen.

12. Have a conversation with the child/children about asking for and/or receiving help and support when one has been left open to the elements and exposed to possible unwelcome experiences. Discuss how it is not something to feel guilty or shameful about, how it is brave to ask for and/or to receive support, and how accepting help leads to a happier and healthier future.

Worry Worms

Purpose:
- Identify and process worries.
- Explore coping strategies.

What you will need:
- *Worry Worms* strips, or colorful construction paper cut into strips
- Markers, google eyes, and decorative materials
- Multiple copies of the *Worry Worms Photo Album* pages

Adult Instructions:

1. Reflect on the previous activities.
2. Provide the child/children with 5-10 construction paper strips, or allow them to cut out the *Worry Worms* strips provided.
3. Model how to fanfold these lengthwise so the strips resemble an inchworm.
4. Allow the child/children to add eyes and decoration to their worms.
5. Explain to the child/children that these are worry worms. Worry worms are squiggly and squirmy, much like the way our body feels when we are worried.
6. Ask the child/children what sort of things they worry about. Take turns sharing your worries.
7. For each worry, pull out one of the worry worms. If you'd like, you can provide names, characteristics, and funny stories about the worry worms. This helps children to externalize, normalize, and add some creative humor and fun to their worries, which may make them less debilitating.
8. Use the worry worms and the descriptions of worries for each to spark conversation about coping mechanisms and strategies to ease worries for each worm. If you'd like, you may pull from the strategies provided in this guide or allow the child/children to brainstorm

their own personal strategies. If you'd like, you can write the worry and/or strategy to calm the worry on the worm itself.

9. You may choose to use the *Worry Worm Photo Album* below as a reflective piece to provide the child/children at the end of this activity. For each worry worm, copy a photo album page and use it as a discussion point. Staple and possibly allow the child/children to illustrate a cover page for the album if you'd like.

*NOTE *Alternate option*

If you'd like, you could also have the child/children paint a plastic bowl to look like a halved apple (red on outside, seeds on the inside) to house their worry worm.

NAME:_____ DATE:_____

Worry Worms

Directions: Cut along solid lines, then fold along the dotted lines, fan-style.

NAME: -SAMPLE-   DATE:_____

Worry Worms Photo Album

Directions: Fill out below.

1. Name: Wilber Wonderworm McWorm-a-worry

2. Worry worm worry: Being home alone at night because mom works late.

3. Worry worm worry traits: Wilber Wonderworm McWorm-a-worry is scared and lonely. He cries a lot and thinks about his mom all the time. His body feels tense and shivery and his heart is sad.

4. How to calm this worry worm: Make a plan with his mom about safe and loving people he can call or have come over when mom is gone. Practice breathing strategies and think of happy things. Do something he likes to keep his mind happy (draw, game, movie).

© 2021, Father Flanagan's Boys' Home

BUILDING RESILIENCY IN CHILDREN

My Seasons

Purpose:

- Understand and accept emotions.
- Identify physiological alerts to emotions and what these alerts mean.
- Determine how to respond to these alerts.

What you will need:

- Scissors
- 1 copy of the *Word Bank of Feelings* for each child
- *My Seasons* page (4 for each child)
- 4 brass brads for each child (found in craft and office supply stores, brass brads are push-pin sized/shaped objects that have a "tail" that splits in order to push through paper and have the ability to turn)

Adult Instructions:

1. Recap the main ideas from the previous activities.

2. Remind the child/children that identifying feelings and emotions, understanding them, and expressing them in a healthy way is important.

3. Remind the child/children that feelings are like the weather and seasons, they come and go. Explain how the seasons are helpful for apples (spring allows for seeds to be planted and begin to grow, summer allows for more growth, fall allows for harvesting, and winter allows for the remaining apples to fall off of the tree and to make room for the new spring batch). Discuss how having different feelings at different times can be a good thing and help us to grow stronger.

4. Using the *Word Bank of Feelings* provided below as a guide, name feelings and discuss them with the child/children.

   NOTE You may ask them to describe this feeling. You may also ask them to explain what this feeling looks/sounds/feels like. If you'd like, you may also ask them to share a time when they have felt this way.

5. Have the child/children circle four words from the *Word Bank* that describe what they feel most often. Write those words in the "I'm..." portion of each green circle.

   NOTE If you would like, you could tell the child/children to draw the weather or a character from the apple read-aloud that reminds them of this feeling under each word in the "I'm..." portion.

© 2021, Father Flanagan's Boys' Home

6. Under the "Feels Like" portion, write words that explain what they feel inside when they are at this place inside.

7. Under the "Looks Like" portion, write words that explain what others might see when the child/children is at this level.

8. Use the "To help this weather pass, I can…" portion to write strategies for overcoming these feelings.

9. Cut out the yellow circle, as well as the triangle "peek" hole.

10. Place the yellow circle over the green and secure with a brass brad in the middle.

11. The child/children may then move the yellow circle around to peek at each portion and to use as needed in each emotion moment.

12. Repeat this activity for all four feelings. Refer to the provided sample for guidance.

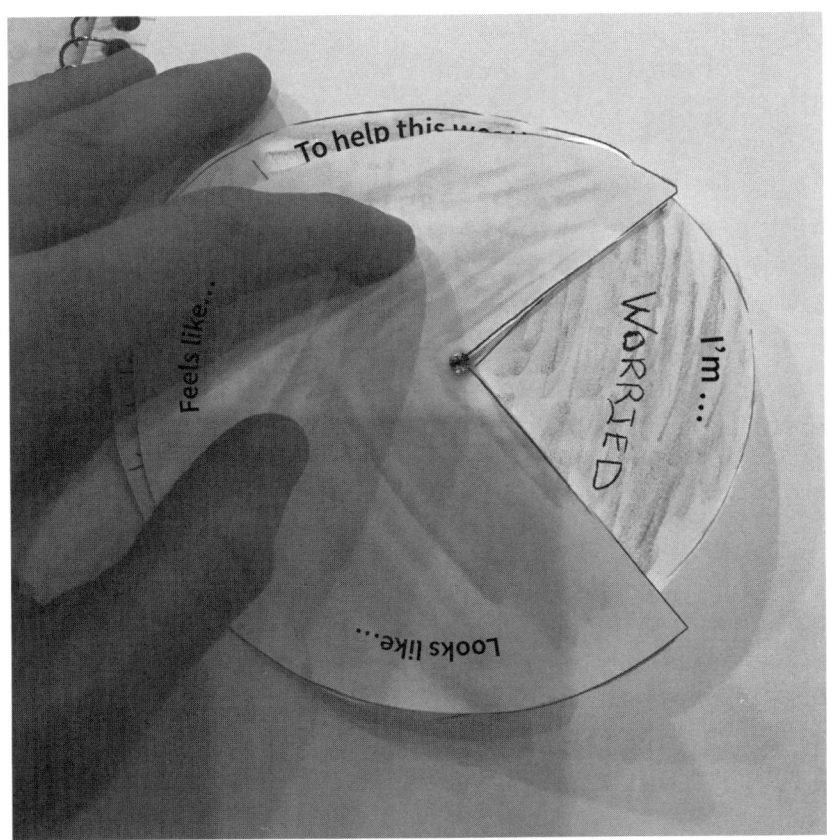

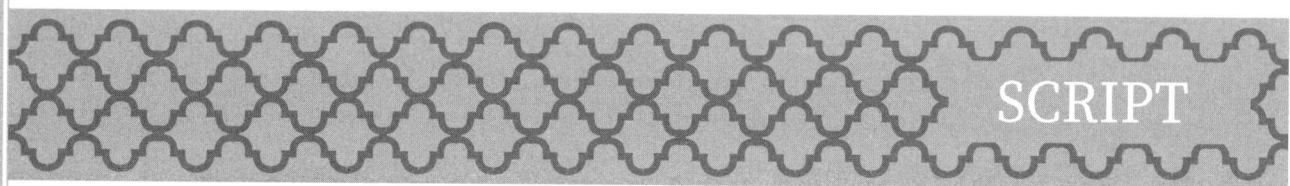

My Seasons Script

Which of these would you expect to see in wintertime?

A snow shower?

An icicle hanging from a roof?

People swimming and hot sunny days?

I'll bet you really wouldn't expect to see people swimming and hot sunny days, would you? You'd expect to see things like sledding and snowflakes! And because you would expect wintertime to be chilly, maybe you'd prepare for it by putting on a coat and gloves before you go outside. Or maybe you warm up with a big mug of hot cocoa.

Just like the weather changes with each season, we all have different feelings at different times and at different levels.

We may have a little sprinkle of rain one day, then a heavy downpour the next. We may have a snow dusting one day, or we may have a blizzard!

It's the same with feelings. We may feel happy sometimes, while at other times, we may feel frustrated! These feelings come and go like the seasons. We may not know exactly why we feel certain ways, and that is okay. It is something we will work on understanding later on in this book. But for now, it is important that we are able to know and to express our feelings.

You wouldn't wear a heavy coat on a summer day, would you? Or a bathing suit in the middle of a snowstorm, right? Just like it is important to know and be prepared for the seasons, it is important to know your feelings and be prepared for them!

In fact, not only is it important that we know what we are feeling, it is important that others around us know what we are feeling, too. When we know what we are feeling, we can better understand how to make ourselves feel better! When we can share how we feel with others, they are able to help us feel better, too!

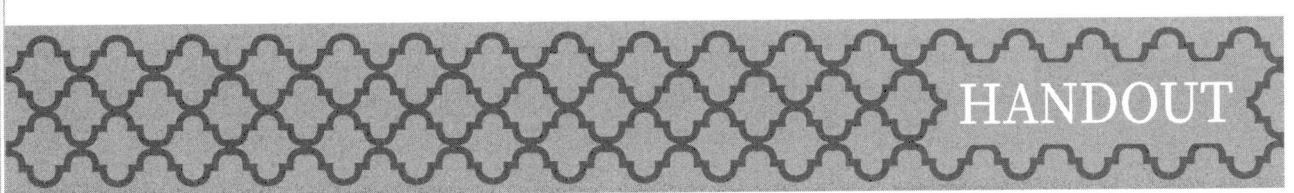

Word Bank of Feelings

happy	worried	ashamed	excited
sad	overwhelmed	uneasy	nervous
mad	furious	frustrated	scared
powerful	grateful	confident	calm
encouraged	relaxed	misunderstood	restless
strong	powerless	inferior	bored

My Seasons

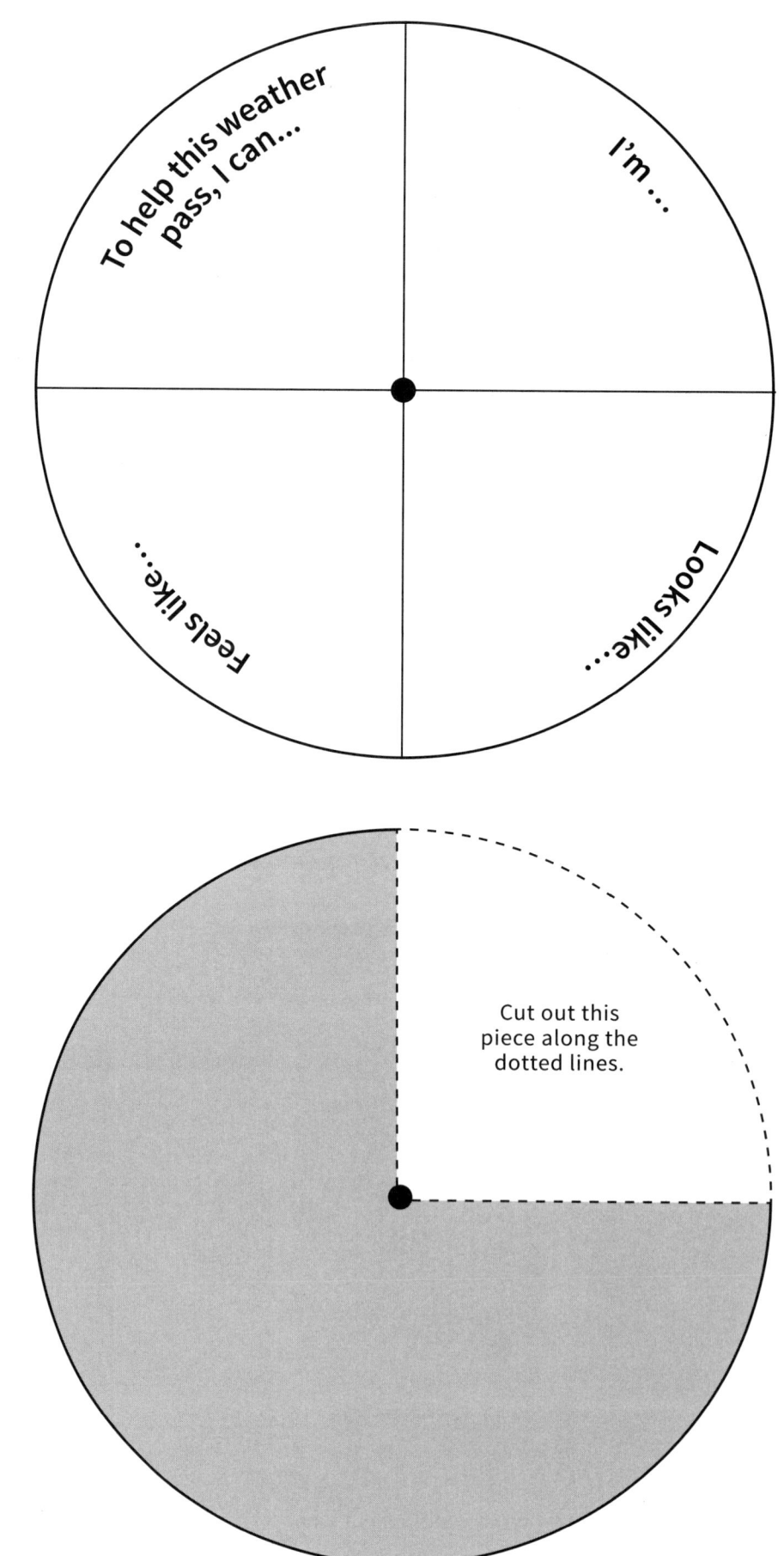

Cut out this piece along the dotted lines.

My Seasons

-SAMPLE-

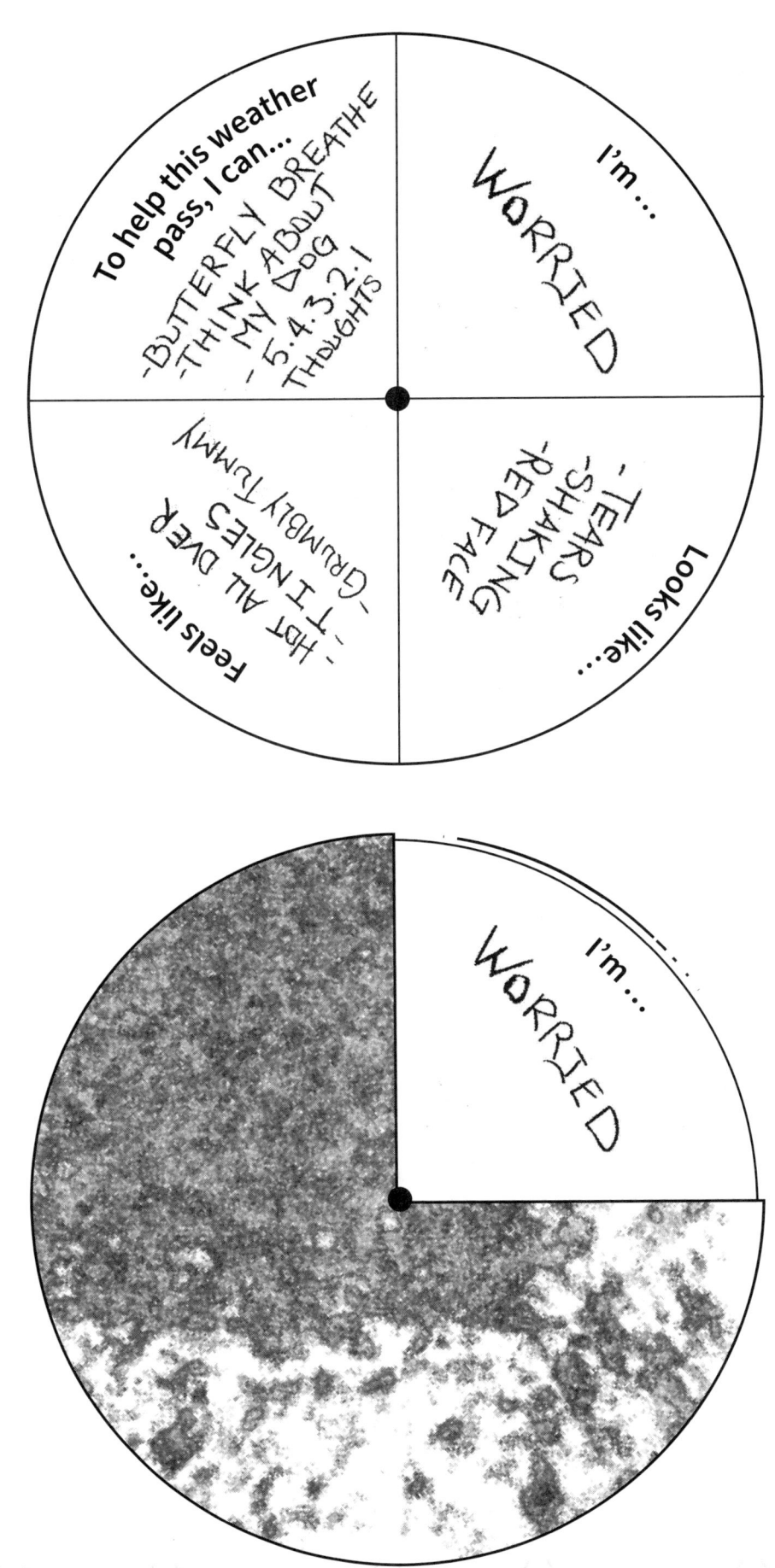

Sample Wording

I'm…	Feels Like…	Looks Like…
Like rain	- A grey cloud is following me - My body is heavy - My head is cloudy - My eyes want to tear up	- Don't want to talk - Not smiling - Slumped over - Misty eyes
Like a blizzard	- Body is tense - Hands are clenched - Teeth are squeezing - I want to jump and kick and scream	- Red face - Balled fists - Screaming - Throwing or hitting
Like a thunderstorm	- Antsy - Jumpy in my tummy - Crawling skin - Tummy ache - Fast heartbeat - Ready to run away	- Tense body - Tears - Closed arms - Heavy breathing
Like a cool spring day, WHERE I WANT TO BE	- Calm - Focused - Normal - Like vanilla ice cream	- Paying attention - Normal body and face - Normal talking

Rotten Apple Pass

Purpose:

- Understand circumstances that lay both in and outside of one's control.
- Recognize the power in response to what lies outside of one's control.

What you will need:

- 1 apple
- Music, an alarm, or another form of a timer

Adult Instructions:

1. Reflect on the previous activities.
2. Explain that today, you will be playing "Rotten Apple Pass."
    a. This game is very much like "Hot Potato."
    b. Each player starts with 10 points.
    c. One person will hold the apple while you turn on the music or alarm.
    d. Pass the apple back and forth until the designated alert goes off.
    e. Whoever is left holding the apple loses a point.
    f. Play until someone reaches "0" points.
3. Discuss control. Explain that there are some things we can control and some things we cannot. For example, you cannot control whether or not you are left holding the rotten apple when the alert goes off, but you can control how you think and respond (telling the other person "good game," telling yourself this is a fun challenge, that you may not be left holding the rotten apple next time, etc.). You may also use another example such as the fact that you cannot control if it will rain, but you can control how you respond to rain by wearing rain boots and a rain jacket, using an umbrella, etc.
4. Brainstorm with the child/children things that they cannot control (examples you may use could include the weather, the way other people think, the way other people act, the way other people feel, what you need to learn in school, etc.).
5. Next, brainstorm things they can control (for example, what to wear to stay comfortable in different types of weather, how they respond to others, the way they think about things that happen/the perception they choose to follow, etc.).
6. Share stories about times when situations were out of your/their control. Brainstorm positive responses (thoughts, words, actions).
7. Discuss how this understanding can help in the future when undesirable experiences arise.

BUILDING RESILIENCY IN CHILDREN

Control to the Core

Purpose:

- Demonstrate the importance and impact of self-control.

What you will need:

- 1 apple
- Space to move/walk around

Adult Instructions:

1. Reflect on the previous activities.
2. Remind the child/children of the last activity and that even though we sometimes cannot control what happens around us, we can control how we respond to situations, and we can control how certain experiences or events impact us.
3. Explain that you will be giving them a challenge today to test their internal control. Tell them they will need to concentrate, focus on their breathing, be patient, move slowly, and work hard to keep control in this challenge.
4. Tell the child/children that they will be placing an apple on their head and that they must walk with it on their head in the designated area (this could be the perimeter of your room, or you could create a mini course using painter's tape or some other form of path identification). The added challenge is they cannot use their hands or anything else to keep the apple balanced. Remind them of the control strategies such as breathing, slow pace and patience, concentrating, and working hard to maintain this balance and focus.
5. Tell the child/children that when they find healthy and positive ways to respond (thoughts, words, actions), they maintain control to the core. They control themselves in every way. Discuss the importance and the power in this type of control, in maintaining focus, and in using tools and strategies to help overcome obstacles.
    a. You could touch on the impact that controlled breathing, mindfulness/focus, and slowing down to think and plan has on the body, the brain, and ultimately on actions, as these strategies create a sense of calm and allow the amygdala (a reactive part of your brain) to get out of "fight, flight, or freeze" mode.
    b. You could discuss action versus reaction and how these strategies help to focus on a healthy and helpful action as opposed to a rushed and unhealthy reaction.
    c. You could explain the overall benefits on mind, body, confidence, and long-term health.

Candy Apple Coat of Armor

Purpose:

- Recognize and identify those people and places that make one feel safe and protected.

What you will need:

- *My Coat of Armor* worksheet
- *Candy Apple Coat of Armor* recipe and ingredients (optional)

Adult Instructions:

1. Reflect on the previous activities.
2. Explain to the child/children that you will be making a special treat today – a candy apple!
3. Follow the recipe below to make the candy-coated apples.
4. Once cooled, ask the child/children to describe the candy apple.
5. Together, discuss the fact that the candy is coated in a hard shell, almost like a coat of armor. Explain that this shell is like protection for the apple. It is much harder to bruise or to bite directly into the apple with this shell protecting it.
6. Discuss what is meant by "coat of armor." Perhaps you could pull up various coats of armor from the internet and share their purpose.
7. Tell the child/children that we all wear invisible coats of armor that help to protect us. Explain that things we armor ourselves in include coping strategies, humor, friends, and supportive loved ones, etc. Discuss the different pieces in your coats of armor and how they help to protect you when things get tough. Ask questions and dig deeper to make a strong conversation out of this activity.
8. (Optional) Work together to create candy apples by following the *Candy Apple Coat of Armor* recipe.
9. Complete the *My Coat of Armor* worksheet as you enjoy the candy apple together.

RECIPE (optional)

Candy Apple Coat of Armor

INGREDIENTS

2-3 apples

Wooden sticks (such as popsicle sticks)

Cocoa, vanilla, or other flavored-candy melts (can be found in grocery or craft stores)

Candy sprinkles, edible glitter, mini-chocolate candies, etc. (optional)

EQUIPMENT

Sheet pan

Microwave

Microwave-safe bowls

DIRECTIONS

1. Wash the apples and remove stems.
2. Insert a wooden stick securely into each apple.
3. Place candy melts in a deep microwave-safe bowl and melt in the microwave according to package directions.
4. Holding the wooden stick, allow the children to dip the apples into their desired candy melts to coat the apples.
5. Once they have finished dipping to their liking, ask them to place the dipped apple onto the sheet pan.
6. If desired, they may decorate the apple with the other edibles (sprinkles, candies, etc.).
7. Allow the candy shell to cool before enjoying.

NAME: _____ DATE: _____

My Coat of Armor

Directions: Below is your coat of armor. In each quadrant, write or draw the people, things, or thoughts that protect you.

Catching the Light

Purpose:

- Recognize how to filter out the bad and keep the positivity/light in any circumstance.

What you will need:

- 1 copy of the *Apple Sun-catcher Stencil*
- 1 paper plate (to be used as the sun-catcher frame)
- Multi-colored tissue paper
- Clear contact paper (making sure than one side remains sticky)
- Scissors

Adult Instructions:

1. **Before meeting,** prepare the sun-catcher frame by cutting the paper plate using the provided stencil as a guide. Fit a piece of contact paper to the plate, being sure that it fills the inside of the sun-catcher (this will be used to hold the tissue paper pieces later).

2. Reflect on the previous activities.

3. Remind the child/children that, even on bad days or in times of unwelcome feelings, there is always something to be grateful for, to feel happy about, or to see the light and color in.

4. Explain how we sometimes need to look very hard, but, when we do, we can always see some light and something positive in our lives.

5. Share stories of when you have looked for something happy, positive, or funny in an otherwise bothersome or frustrating experience (such as an opportunity for growth, to shift your mindset on an experience, to help others, etc.).

6. Reflect on the previous discussions about things that make the child/children feel happy and things they are grateful for.

7. Tell the child/children that today, they will be focusing on the light and happy things. Tell them you will be creating a colorful sun-catcher. Discuss what a sun-catcher is, what it does, and how it uses light to add to its beauty.

8. Allow the child/children to use multi-colored tissue papers to cut out various shapes and sizes. Tell them they will use these pieces to fill in the frame and remind them they may want to consider the sizes they use based on the space inside of the frame.

9. Ask the child/children to arrange the tissue paper inside of the apple frame, being careful to not let too much tissue paper overlap, as this will limit the amount of light it can catch.

10. For each piece they lay down, ask them to either share:
    a. One thing that brings light to them/makes them happy
    b. One way they can find light in an unwelcome situation

11. Once they have finished, tie or glue the sun-catcher to a window. Take a moment to discuss the beauty of the sun-catcher and how it filters in colorful light. Use this to prompt discussion about the importance of finding happiness, light, and color in situations that we may not always be happy about.

Apple Sun-catcher Stencil

Ugly Apple Head

Purpose:

- Demonstrate how to turn something "ugly" (such as a bad experience) into something beautiful, positive, or into an opportunity.

What you will need:

- 1 apple
- Markers
- 1 paring knife
- Salt
- Lemon juice
- Equipment
- Baking sheet
- Oven

Adult Instructions:

1. Prep for the activity by peeling and coring the apple.
2. Reflect on previous activities with the child/children.
3. Remind them that, sometimes, we have to search very hard to find the good in a situation or experience, but that focusing on the good makes us stronger, happier, and promotes our overall wellness.
4. Discuss times when you have had to see the good or cool aspects of something gone wrong. This can be a moment where you demonstrated bravery, where you helped someone else, where you learned something, where you kept going and demonstrated grit/perseverance, etc.
5. Hand the peeled and cored apple to the child/children. Ask them to use the marker to draw a face.

6. Once they have finished, ask them to pour or dip the apple in lemon juice until the apple is coated.

7. Ask them to pour salt onto the baking sheet in an even pile.

8. Meanwhile, use the paring knife to cut out the face that they had drawn.

9. Ask the child/children to place the apple in the middle of the baking sheet on top of the salt.

10. Bake the apple at 180 degrees overnight.

11. Come back and share observations with them.

12. Discuss how the wrinkled apple head could be seen as a negative, as it is not crispy and fresh like it was the previous day, then share a conversation about what makes the wrinkled version cool and unique.

13. Reflect on how to use this idea in real life/how to shift your perspective in order to turn a negative into a positive.

Some ideas include:
   a. Growing stronger or wiser from an experience
   b. Helping others during an unpleasant experience
   c. Demonstrating bravery, grit, care, perseverance
   d. Using an experience to teach others
   e. Using your creativity to self-soothe and to shift your narrative in an experience

Shape Shifting Apple Art

Purpose:

- Identify how to shift thoughts in order to see something in a new and more positive light.

What you will need:

- *Shape Shift Apple Art* worksheet
- Writing/coloring utensils

Adult Instructions:

1. Reflect on the previous activities.
2. Remind the child/children that we sometimes need to search for the light and positivity in things that we experience, but that there is always something good that can come out of each moment.
3. Tell the child/children that, today, they will be using their creativity and imagination to create something new out of an apple shape. Tell them that they will demonstrate seeing things in a new light by making something completely different out of the original shape.
4. Share ideas (ladybug, heart, face, animal, paint palette, flower, strawberry, bird, lollipop, etc.).
5. Allow the child/children to draw, add, create, and have fun completing the *Shape Shift Apple Art* worksheet.
6. When they have finished, discuss what they created and how they can use this imaginative mindset to find the good in unwelcome experiences. Identify how creatively shifting thoughts on various experiences helps us to learn, grow, see the good, and feel happier overall.

NAME:_____   DATE:_____

Shape Shifting Apple Art

Directions: Use your creativity and imagination to create something new out of an apple shape. You will be seeing things in a new light by making something completely different out of the original shape. Please draw, add, create, and have fun completing the worksheet.

Coping, Grounding, and Calming

Once children and adolescents are empowered with the ability to process emotions in a healthy way, they can then focus on tending to and coping with negative or unpleasant experiences. The application of grounding techniques and healthy coping mechanisms is paramount in overcoming trauma and increasing overall well-being.

The activities in this section are designed to allow for the exploration of various coping tools and techniques. They are vast enough to touch on distinct styles and areas of interest. It is the hope that these activities will illuminate unique strengths and curiosities, which can then be used to create individualized coping plans that suit specific needs.

BUILDING RESILIENCY IN CHILDREN

Apple Senses

Purpose:

- Identify the 5 senses.
- Focus on the senses as a means of self-soothing.

What you will need:

- 1 apple, sliced

Adult Instructions:

1. Reflect on previous activities.
2. Ask the child/children if they can tell you what our five senses are. Prompt them if necessary.
3. Tell the child/children that our senses can act as a source of comfort when we are experiencing unwelcome feelings. Explain that focusing on our senses, one at a time, anywhere and at any time, can help us to feel calm and to redirect our focus away from the unwelcome feelings. That way, we can respond in a way that allows us to feel better and to maintain control.
4. Tell the child/children that they will be practicing how to focus on their senses today.
5. Give them the apple.
6. Ask the child/children to describe what they see (color, shape, surrounding, details, etc.).
7. Ask the child/children to shift their focus onto touch. Tell them to pick up an apple slice. If they'd like to close their eyes in order to hone in on touch, they may.
8. Ask the child/children to describe what they feel (cool, sticky, moist, hard, smooth, etc.).

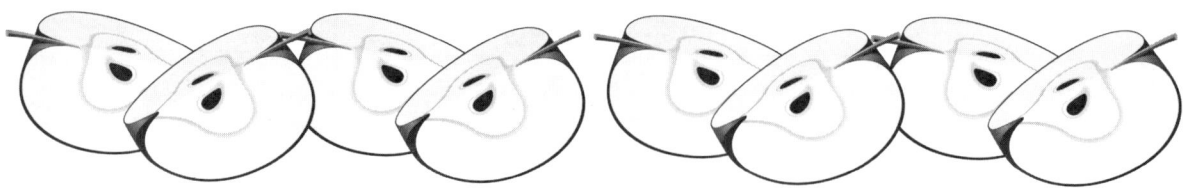

9. Ask the child/children to now shift their focus on smell. They may choose to keep their eyes closed for this.
10. Ask the child/children to describe what they smell (sweet, fresh, outdoor, fruity, etc.).
11. Ask the child/children to now shift their focus on taste and sound. They may choose to keep their eyes closed for this.
12. They may now take a bite into the apple slice.
13. Ask the child/children to describe what they taste (sweet, juicy, tart, crisp, crunchy, etc.).
14. Ask the child/children to describe what they hear as they chew.
15. Discuss how this is a powerful tool that can be used at anytime and anywhere. Whenever they feel the need to shift their focus or to distract their minds, they can focus on their senses.
16. Remind them to ask themselves questions like:
    a. What do I see around me? They can focus on an object or on many.
    b. What do I smell? Does this smell remind me of anything?
    c. What do I hear? Even if they only hear the sound of wind or a clock.
    d. What do I feel? This can be temperature, an object they are holding, the seat or floor they are sitting on, etc.
    e. What do I taste? If they have something in their mouths.

Apple Dumpling

Purpose:

- Practice grounding, self-soothing, and reflecting on people, places, and/or things that youth can refer back to in times they need to calm.

What you will need:

- A warm and comfortable blanket
- One *Apple Dumpling* worksheet
  NOTE: You may also choose to create the same activity using play dough, soft felt paper, or any other craft medium
- (Optional) Ingredients for apple dumpling recipe (below), if you'd prefer
- One copy of the *Guided Visualization* process

Adult Instructions:

1. Ask the child/children if they have ever seen/tasted an apple dumpling.

2. If the child/children have seen/tasted an apple dumpling, ask them to describe what it looks like. If they have not, explain what an apple dumpling is. Try to show them pictures, if possible.

3. Remind the child/children that an apple dumpling is a spiced and sweetened apple wrapped up in a blanket of sweet dough, then baked to create a warm and delicious treat.

4. Complete the *Apple Dumpling* worksheet with the child/children.

5. Lead the child/children through the *Guided Visualization* process. To start, place the blanket on the floor. As you read the paragraph starting with: "Feel the gentle hands that softly lift you up and lay you in the middle of this comfortable airy blanket of dough..." Be sure to allow the child/children the opportunity to roll onto the blanket and envelope snuggly inside, as if they are the apple being blanketed by the dumpling dough.

6. Once you have completed the guided visualization, use the questions as prompts to discuss how mini-mind vacations can be used at any time to calm and ground themselves when they are feeling elevated.

Apple Dumpling

Directions:

1. Allow the child/children to color and cut out both the apple and the dumpling sheet.

2. Next, ask them to place the apple in the middle of the dumpling sheet.

3. On each corner of the dumpling sheet, they may write or draw one mini-mind vacation that they can take when they need a moment away. This can be something silly, like making themselves into an apple dumpling or pretending that they are a unicorn riding on cotton-candy clouds, or they can make it a place that they feel the most comfortable and warm, like the swing set at their favorite park or at their favorite restaurant.

4. Fold each corner of the dumpling sheet up so that it blankets the apple.

5. Explain to the child/children that they can carry this with them as a reminder of the things that make them feel warm, loved, safe, and happy. Tell them to think of these things whenever they feel anything undesirable.

PROCESS

Guided Visualization

Get into a position that is comfortable for you. Maybe you want to lay on your back or stomach. Maybe you want to sit and put your head down. You may notice that there is a blanket unfolded on the ground as well. We will be using this blanket later on.

Close your eyes and take a slow, deep breath. The kind of breath you take when you smell a fresh batch of ooey, gooey apple dumplings getting pulled from the oven.

Slowly in through your nose.

Slowly out through your mouth.

Keeping your eyes closed and your breaths slow and deep.

Let's take a mini vacation in our minds. We are going to pretend that you are somewhere else and something else. I am going to guide you through this mini vacation with my words. As I speak, I want you to keep your eyes closed and try to imagine my words as a movie in your mind. Try to picture the story as you hear it. Try to imagine this story as if you were living it.

Imagine that you are an apple. A sweet, crisp apple freshly picked from your tree. Feel the cool, crisp orchard air on your skin. Imagine how fun the ride would be as you get plucked from your tree, placed in a basket, and walked to the front porch of a farmhouse. Try to imagine what you would see along the way. Would you see mountains? Fields? Farm animals? What would you hear? Would you feel the wind whistling by? Would you hear the farmer whistling a happy tune? Would you hear the farm animals chattering and galloping?

Let's keep breathing.

Slowly in through your nose.

Slowly out through your mouth.

Now, imagine that you have been gently placed onto the kitchen table. Can you feel the smooth and cool table beneath you?

You watch as flour, sugar, milk, and eggs get mixed, kneaded, and rolled into a soft and pillowy blanket for you.

Feel the gentle hands that softly lift you up and lay you in the middle of this comfortable, airy blanket of dough.

NOTE *At this point, you may stop and ask the child/children if they would like to roll into the blanket and wrap themselves into it.*

Smell the warmth of cinnamon and sugar as it sprinkles over you like sweet and spicy snowflakes. Feel the softness of the dumpling blanketing over you, protecting you.

DISCUSS

Discussion/Follow Up:

Once the child/children have opened their eyes and are ready to talk, ask them:

- Does your body feel differently now than when we first started the story?
- What does your body feel like now?
- How did the deep breaths make you feel?
- How did sitting comfortably with your eyes closed make you feel?
- How do you think breathing and sitting like this could help you in times that you feel sad, angry, or upset?

Next, move on to the story.

- How did you feel as you imagined?
- How did you feel once you were wrapped in your warm, dumpling-dough blanket?
- What made you feel this way?
- Pretend that you have a cozy cocoon of your own. You can close your eyes if it helps you to create a picture in your mind. Describe your cozy cocoon to me.
- What do you see inside of your cozy cocoon (colors, items, people, etc.)?
- What do you hear inside of your cozy cocoon (music, nature, etc.)?
- What do you feel inside of your cozy cocoon (soft, fuzzy, warmth, etc.)?
- What do you smell inside of your cozy cocoon (vanilla, cake, etc.)?

RECIPE
(optional)

Apple Dumpling Recipe

INGREDIENTS

1 ½ c. sugar
½ c. brown sugar
2 c. water
½ stick of butter
1 tbsp cinnamon
1 tbsp vanilla
1 can premade pie crust or crescent dough
4 apples, peeled and cored

EQUIPMENT

1 large casserole/sheet pan with sides
1 saucepan
1 large spoon

DIRECTIONS

1. Preheat oven according to the package of dough chosen.
2. In a saucepan, bring water, butter, and sugars to a boil.
3. Heat until sugars dissolve, then take off the heat source (remember to turn the stove off, as well).
4. Add cinnamon and vanilla, then set aside.
5. Lay dough flat on the sheet pan. If using crescent dough, arrange triangles so that they create 4 large squares. If using pie dough, cut into 4 squares.
6. Place one peeled and cored apple in the middle of each dough square.
7. Fold each corner of dough up and allow them to meet at the top of the apple.

Apple Dumpling Recipe (continued)

8. Pinch the corners together and use your hands to pinch dough around any bare spots where the apple can be seen. Do your best to blanket the entire apple in dough.
9. Carefully pour the sugar mixture over and around the blanketed dumplings.
10. Bake according to directions on the dough package. You may need to bake a few minutes longer due to the sugar mixture and the moistness of the apples. If the bottom of the dumplings look underdone when you take them out, continue to bake in 5 minute increments until fully cooked.
11. Allow to cool before enjoying it with a scoop of ice cream, whipped cream, or plain!

BUILDING RESILIENCY IN CHILDREN

Sock Worm Buddy

Purpose:

- Create and use a calming and comforting keepsake.

What you will need:

- 1 clean sock, preferably a plain knee-length sock
- Google-eyes, markers, and other decorative items
- Uncooked rice or beans
- Needle and thread (if sewing the sock shut is desired)
- Calming essential oils such as lavender, vanilla, cinnamon, etc.

Adult Instructions:

1. Reflect on previous activities.
2. Allow the child/children to decorate the worm as they would like. You may let them know that the toe-end will serve as the worm face. You can suggest adding eyes, a mouth, decoration, etc.
3. Using a cup, funnel, or other tool, carefully pour the dried rice or beans into the sock until it is about 3/4 full.
4. Place a few drops of essential oil in and massage/roll/squeeze the sock, allowing the oil to cover a good amount of the rice or beans.
5. Sew or tie the open end of the sock shut.
6. Explain that focusing on the feel and scent of the worm buddy helps ease you when you feel angry, sad, scared, etc.
7. Model various ways to use this worm buddy:
    a. Sniffing the calming scent
    b. Squeezing, hugging, or rolling the worm buddy with your hands or feet
    c. Placing the worm buddy on your neck, lap, shoulders, legs, arms, back, etc. to feel the weight
    d. Warming the worm buddy in the microwave for 20 seconds also creates a warming sensation and increases the oil scent
8. Discuss times when the child/children could use their worm buddy.

Cortland's Warm & Cozy Cider Secret

Purpose:
- Practice a multitude of grounding techniques.

What you will need:
- Recipe and ingredients

Adult Instructions:

1. Reflect on the previous activities.
2. Re-read, or have a quick recap discussion of the read-aloud.
3. Remind the child/children that when we have unwelcome feelings, it can be helpful to focus our minds and bodies on soothing things. Remind them how calming our bodies allows our minds to calm down as well, and that this can make us feel better.
4. Tell the child/children that you will be practicing ways to think about warm and cozy things in order to calm our bodies and minds. Tell them you will use your imagination, as well as your five senses, to soothe and to find a calm place in your minds.
5. Reflect on the five senses and how to focus on one sense at a time.
6. Use the included recipe to make Cortland's Famous Cinnamon Spiced Cider.
7. Pour a cup of cider for both you and the child/children. Before they take a sip, practice using their senses and provide them with a mindful breathing strategy. After you hand them their cup of cider, ask them to close their eyes. You may use the following prompts:
    a. Feel the warmth of the cup in your hands. Focus on this sensation.
    b. Lean closer to the cup of cider. Can you feel the steam coming up from the cup and tickling your face?

    c. Keeping your eyes closed, take a slow deep whiff of the cider. Be sure to breathe slowly in through your nose and try to focus only on the sweet and spicy warm scent. Keep your mind on warm and cozy feelings and memories.
    d. As you slowly exhale out of your mouth, imagine all of your worries, fears, frustrations, floating away with the steam coming off of the cider as you blow.
    e. Slowly breathe in again, focusing on the warmth, scent, and things that make you feel warm and cozy.
    f. Slowly exhale and blow any unwelcome feelings away with your breath.
    g. You may slowly inhale and exhale once more if you'd like.
    h. How does this warmth, this scent, this breathing make you feel? Try to capture this feeling.

8. Tell the child/children they can do this even in moments when they do not have cider. They can cup their hands together and use their imagination to picture themselves holding Cortland's Famous Spiced cider, a mug of hot cocoa, a cool and creamy milkshake, or any other comforting treat that they may desire. Model how to use your imagination by slowly inhaling, imagine smelling the treat and feeling the warmth or coolness, slowly exhaling away the unwelcome feelings, and repeating.

9. Reflect on how this exercise makes the child/children feel. Discuss times that this could come in handy.

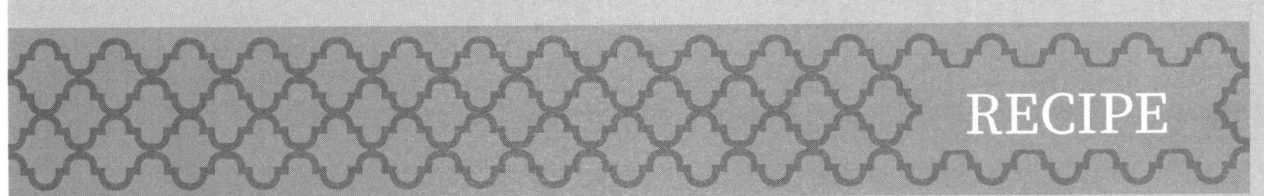

Cortland's Famous Cinnamon Spiced Cider Recipe

INGREDIENTS

One quart of apple cider (or juice, if you cannot find cider)

1 tsp orange rind

1 tbsp cinnamon

1 tsp nutmeg

1 pinch ground cloves

¼ c. brown sugar

EQUIPMENT

1 large pot

DIRECTIONS

1. Carefully pour apple cider/juice into a pot.
2. Add brown sugar and spices.
3. Place on the stove and stir until sugar dissolves.
4. Heat to taste.
5. Gently pour into mugs.
6. If desired, garnish with a cinnamon stick or orange slice.

BUILDING RESILIENCY IN CHILDREN

Apple Finger Maze Breathing

Purpose:

- Practice simple grounding activities.

What you will need:

- One copy of *Apple Finger Mazes*

Adult Instructions:

1. Reflect on the previous activities.
2. Remind the child/children that one helpful way to decrease unwelcome feelings is to use strategies that calm them. Discuss some of the calming strategies that you have explored so far, which they like the best, and when they have used them outside of their time with you.
3. Explain to the child/children that you will be practicing another technique for calming down in moments that they can use when they need to feel better.
4. Tell them that today's technique involves breathing and tracing. Remind them how breathing is a powerful tool for calming their minds, bodies, and preparing their brains to respond to unwelcome situations in a positive way.
5. Show the *Apple Finger Mazes* to the child/children. Tell them that they will connect finger movements with their breathing today. That focusing on this connection will help their brains and bodies to feel calmed and soothed when they are having any unwelcome feelings.
6. Model how to slowly inhale as you allow your finger to follow the path of the apple maze, and exhale as you round the apple curve into the next section. Follow the maze slowly with your finger, connecting your movements to your breath.
7. Allow the child/children to practice this, as well.
8. If you'd like, you can allow the child/children to create their own finger maze inside of the empty heart shape.

NAME: _____   DATE: _____

Apple Finger Mazes

Directions: Use your finger to complete these mazes. Use the empty heart below to create one of your own, and have a friend complete it.

BUILDING RESILIENCY IN CHILDREN

Grounding Apple Pendulum

Purpose:

- Practice a simple grounding technique.

What you will need:

- One piece of string or yarn (about 12-15 inches in length)
- One nut (to be found at the hardware store)
- Red or green paint (apple colored)
- Red or green glitter (apple colored)
- Paint brushes

Adult Instructions:

1. Reflect on previous activities.

2. Remind the child/children that one helpful way to decrease unwelcome feelings is to use strategies that calm them. Discuss some of the calming strategies that you have explored so far, which they like the best, and when they have used them outside of their time with you.

3. Explain to the child/children that you will be practicing another technique for calming down in moments when they need to feel better.

4. Tell the child/children that today's technique involves breathing, timing, and allowing their minds to drift. Remind them how breathing is a powerful tool for calming their minds, bodies, and preparing their brains to respond to unwelcome situations in a positive way.

5. If already completed, discuss how the apple finger mazes were practice for connecting timing to breathing, as connecting finger movements to breaths somewhat requires paying attention to time and making that connection.

6. Tell the child/children that in order to complete today's activity, they must first make a tool that allows them to focus on timing and on mind drifting.

7. Give the child/children time to paint the nut using apple-colored paints and glitter. Once this has dried, tie the nut to the end of the string to create a pendulum.

8. If you'd like, you may take a moment to explain the purpose and science of pendulums.

9. Ask the child/children if they know what "drifting" means, or what it means to allow their mind to drift. Give examples, if needed.

10. Explain that sometimes our minds get filled with unwelcome thoughts – so filled that they sometimes seem like they are overflowing and there is no way to stop them. In those moments, we need to let our minds drift away – away from the unwelcome thoughts and toward more positive things.

11. Allow the pendulum to move in a gentle swaying motion.

12. Explain to the child/children that you are going to focus on two things:
    a. The swing and sway of the pendulum
    b. The way your breathing sways with the pendulum

13. Model breathing slowly in through your nose for 3 full swings, then out through your mouth for 4 full swings. Count with them as you model (in 1-2-3, out 1-2-3-4). Using a calm tone, remind them that you are letting the pendulum and your breathing maintain your focus, as everything else drifts out of your mind. Nothing but you, your breath, and the sway of the pendulum.

14. Allow the child/children to hold the pendulum and practice. Start by practicing with them before giving them the opportunity to practice on their own.

15. Once finished, reflect on how the child/children feel. How did they feel as they were connecting their breath to the pendulum sways? When could they use this outside of your time with them?

BUILDING RESILIENCY IN CHILDREN

Progressive Muscle Relaxation (PMR)

Purpose:

- Practice simple grounding activities.

What you will need:

- Space to move
- *PMR Visual*
- *PMR Prompt*

Adult Instructions:

1. Reflect on previous activities.
2. Remind the child/children that when we experience unwelcome feelings or when our brains are overflowing with undesirable thoughts, it helps to relax our bodies. Remind them that we do this through our breathing and movements.

3. Tell the child/children that today, you will be practicing a way to calm your body and your mind through a movement story.
4. Tell them that you will be using a tool called "Progressive Muscle Relaxation," or PMR, in which you focus on making parts of your body tense up as you slowly breathe in, then release the tension as you breathe out. You can focus on the relaxing, tingly feeling that this tension release creates.
5. Display the visual as a guide.
6. Tell them to follow along with your words as, together, you use PMR to act out an orchard tale.
7. Read the prompt and act these motions out with the child/children.
8. When finished, reflect on:
    a. how this activity felt in the moment,
    b. how focusing on tension and release calms your body, and
    c. when this would be helpful outside of your time with them.

PMR Visual

PROCESS

PMR Prompt

Imagine we are standing in the middle of an apple orchard. Listen to the leaves rustling in the wind. Feel the warmth of the sunshine on your cheeks. Can you smell the sweet apples growing all around you?

Let's pretend like we have a handful of apple seeds to plant. To make this even more fun, let's pretend like we cannot use our hands to plant these seeds. In fact, the only thing we can use to plant them... is our feet!

Kick your shoes off and let's get planting!

First, we need to dig a little hole, or divot, in the dirt. Let's use our heels and the pads of our feet to twist, twist, twist a hole in the dirt. Breathing in, move your heels and pads in a twisting motion. Continue for 7 seconds.

Breathe out as you relax your feet.

Now, we need to plant the seeds. Toss them into the divot you just made in the dirt. Breathe in as you use your toes to really pack the seeds tightly in the dirt. Wiggle your toes to drive the seeds down further. Continue for 7 seconds.

Breathe out as you relax your toes.

Next, let's pretend to be the seedling as it sprouts into a mighty apple tree. Breathe in as you crouch down and hug your legs. Try to pack your body into a seed shape. Hold this position for 7 seconds.

Breathe out as you slowly sprout up, taller and taller.

Breathe in as you stretch as tall as you can, reaching your arms to the sky to become the tallest tree in the orchard. Hold this position for 7 seconds.

Breathe out as you stretch your arms wide, like they are branches. Breathe in and hold this position for 7 seconds.

Breathe out as you relax your body and let your arms fall to the side.

We are now going to pretend that we are little green worms, hungry for a taste of the delicious apples growing in this orchard. Wriggle your body like a worm until you reach the apple you'd like to munch into. Once you find it, breathe in and move your jaws back and forth, up and down, in a circle motion, as if you

PMR Promt (continued)

are munch, munch, munching away and creating a tunnel in an apple with each taste. Continue for 7 seconds.

Breathe out as you relax your jaw.

Now, you want to move through the tunnel that you've created inside of this juicy apple. Breathe in as you suck your stomach in. Suck in as if you are trying to squeeze through a tight spot. Hold for 7 seconds.

Breathe out as you relax your stomach.

Let's do our best impression of an apple! Breathe in and hold, allowing your cheeks to puff out with the air you're holding inside. You now have apple cheeks!

Breathe out as you rest your cheeks.

Lastly, let's make some apple juice. Pretend like you have an apple in each hand. Now, squeeze, squeeze, squeeze as hard as you can! Breathe in slowly as you squeeze all of the juice out of the apples! Squeeze, squeeze, squeeze, don't stop squeezing…

PHEW! Ok, you got all of the juice out. Good job. Now, take a slow breath out as you release the apples.

Worm Wriggle

Purpose:

- Practice simple calming movement techniques.

What you will need:

- Space to move in
- *Worm Wriggle Prompt*

Adult Instructions:

1. Reflect on previous activities.
2. Engage the child/children in a discussion about the power of breathing and movement. Discuss when to use breathing and movement, how they help calm and ground us, and ask for any moments that breathing and movement have helped since starting these sessions.
3. Tell the child/children that, today, you will be practicing a way to calm your body and mind through breathing and movement.
4. Tell them that you will be stretching and moving your body in a fun way. Explain that the purpose of this will be to focus on:
    a. movement,
    b. connecting your breathing with movement,
    c. stretching your body to make it feel calm and eased, and
    d. having fun and being silly (because fun and giggles are also powerful tools in countering negative or unwelcome feelings and emotions).
5. Tell child/children to follow along with your words as, together, you wriggle like inchworms in an apple orchard.
6. Read the *Worm Wriggle* prompt and act these motions out with the child/children.
7. When finished, reflect on:
    a. how stretching and wriggling like a worm felt,
    b. how stretching and slow movements can calm your body and mind,
    c. how a little fun and silliness can make you feel better, and
    d. when this would be helpful outside of your time with the child/children.

PROCESS

Worm Wriggle Prompt

1. Consider how an inchworm moves... slow and steady. Try to keep your movements slow and steady like an inchworm.

2. Stand up and take a deep breath in, then a deep breath out.

3. Take another deep breath in as you put your feet together and place your hands on your side.

4. Keeping your feet together and your knees straight, breathe out as you bend forward from your waist, stretching down, allowing your body to dangle.

5. Pay attention to how this makes your legs, back, and arms feel. Do they feel like they are being gently pulled?

6. Take a deep breath in as you slowly extend your arms out and allow them to touch the ground, all the while keeping your legs straight. Your body should look like a tent when you are done.

7. Take a deep breath in and out as you focus on which parts of your body feel like they are being gently stretched and pulled.

8. Now, here comes the really fun part! We are going to move like an inchworm!

9. Try to move both feet forward, as close to your hands as possible. Take a deep breath in before moving your hands forward, so that your body looks like a tent again.

10. Breathe out.

11. Continue moving in this pattern, feet to hands, hands forward, like an inchworm. All the while, focusing on:
    - breathing in and out, slowly and calmly like a worm
    - which parts of your body are being gently stretched and pulled

12. Once you are wriggle wormed out, stop, sit comfortably or stand, and let's reflect on how stretching and breathing can help us when we need to be calm.

BUILDING RESILIENCY IN CHILDREN

Squeezable Comforting Apple Pie

Purpose:
- Create and use a self-soothing sensory keepsake.

What you will need:
- Recipe and ingredients

Adult Instructions:
1. Reflect on previous activities.
2. Remind the child/children that when we experience unwelcome feelings or when our brains are overflowing with undesirable thoughts, it helps to relax our bodies and to let our minds drift or focus on our senses in the present.
3. Tell the child/children that you will be making something that will help to calm and soothe them – something fun that will allow them to focus on their senses as they mold, squish, smell, and create… soothing apple pie dough!
4. Make the apple pie dough with the child/children (remind them not to eat it).
5. Allow them time to play with the dough before prompting them to focus on their senses with questions and comments such as:
    a. Yum, doesn't this dough smell good? What does that scent remind you of?
    b. What does the dough feel like between your fingers?
    c. What is your favorite way to use this dough so far? Squishing? Molding? Rolling?
    d. What does this dough look like to you? What shape are you making it into?
6. When finished, reflect on how they feel as they use the dough, how they felt making the dough, and when using this (or another form of dough/clay/slime) would be helpful outside of your time with them.

RECIPE

Soothing Apple Pie Dough Recipe

INGREDIENTS

2 c. cinnamon

2 c. applesauce

½ c. white glue

Additional dry ingredient such as flour or cornstarch, if needed

EQUIPMENT

1 large bowl

1 spoon (or get super sensory and just use your hands!)

DIRECTIONS

1. Dump the cinnamon into the bowl.
2. Spoon the applesauce into the bowl.
3. Pour the glue into the bowl.
4. Using the spoon or your hands, combine the ingredients until they form a dough-like consistency. If needed, you may add the additional dry ingredient.
5. Once you have reached your desired consistency, you may use this dough to squeeze, mold, shape, or sniff. Practice being mindful of your senses as you play with the dough (focus on the feels as you squeeze, as you roll, what it smells like, etc.). Have fun!
6. You may leave the dough out to dry or choose to keep in a baggie or airtight container for future use.

Boosting B.I.N.G.O.

Purpose:

- Explore a variety of grounding, calming, and coping strategies.
- Reflect and create a personal plan for self-soothing and coping.

What you will need:

- *Boosting B.I.N.G.O.* board *(one different one for each child)*
- One *Boosting B.I.N.G.O.* card cut so that strategies can be drawn in bingo game
- Blank 4x4 box card
- Marker, crayon, pencil, pen, or other writing utensil

Adult Instructions:

1. Before meeting, cut apart individual strategies for one card.
2. Reflect on previous activities.
3. Ask the child/children if they have ever played bingo.
4. If they have, ask them to remind you of the rules. If they have not, explain the rules to them.
5. Pass out a *Boosting B.I.N.G.O.* board to the child/children. Explain that each box contains an activity. Tell them these the activities are tools they can use when they start to feel applesauced, stinky, or have unwelcome feelings that make them feel fuzzy and flooded.
6. Go over the activities in each box (see explanations and examples in the "Snap Skills" section of the *Building Resiliency in Youth* guide).
7. Tell the child/children you will be playing a game of bingo with these mood-boosting and grounding activities.
8. Draw a strategy card and model it or have a volunteer model it. Keep going until game is complete.
9. Pass out a blank 4x4 box card to each child. Tell them you will help them fill out their card to use when they need it.

A Trauma-Informed Activity Guide for Children

10. Over the course of the next week or so, have the child/children alert you when their fuzzy and flooded alarms are sounding. Pull out the board and have them choose an activity to calm and soothe them. Do this activity with them until they are ready to reflect and to move forward with a positive and energized day. Have them record the activity on their card if it works for them.

11. Possible questions to ask after each activity is completed:
    a. What are you feeling now?
    b. Did this activity help you?
    c. What did you like the most about this activity?
    d. Can you see yourself using this activity in other times that you feel fuzzy and flooded?
    e. Would you recommend this activity to a friend who is feeling fuzzy and flooded?

12. Keep the cards handy and use the strategies with the child/children as needed.

BUILDING RESILIENCY IN CHILDREN

Munching Unwelcome Feelings Away

Purpose:
- Reflect on coping strategies and determine which work best for the individual.
- Create a visual reminder of these strategies.

What you will need:
- *Munching Unwelcome Feelings Away* activity sheet
- Crayons, makers, pencils
- Scissors
- 1 brass brad (per child)

Adult Instructions:

1. Reflect on previous activities.
2. Expand on the discussion by asking the child/children which of the strategies explored so far seem to have the best impact on them. If needed, remind them of the activities explored and discuss each in a "list and reflect" manner.
3. Make note of their favorite strategies.
4. Tell the child/children that, today, you will be creating a tool that will help them to remember the activities and strategies they prefer the most.
5. Remind them that, sometimes, our unwelcome thoughts and feelings can take over and we cannot think of ways to ease them. That is where *Munching Unwelcome Feelings Away* tool comes in! Explain this will serve as a reminder, and a choice-maker, of which strategy to use in these moments.
6. In each section of the circle, write one of the child's preferred strategies. Be sure to write a strategy in each section. (If completing activity with multiple children, each child will create one.)
7. Allow time to color the circle, apple, and worm.
8. Cut the circle and apple out.
9. Align the dots in the center of the apple and the circle up, piercing both with the brass brad. Be sure that the circle is placed behind the apple, words facing the front.
10. Fold the arms of the brad back, securing the tool.
11. Model how to use this tool (the brass brad will act as a spinner, allowing you to move the strategies into view, one at a time, through the bitten portion of the apple).
12. Discuss when this tool would be useful.

A Trauma-Informed Activity Guide for Children

Munching Unwelcome Feelings Away

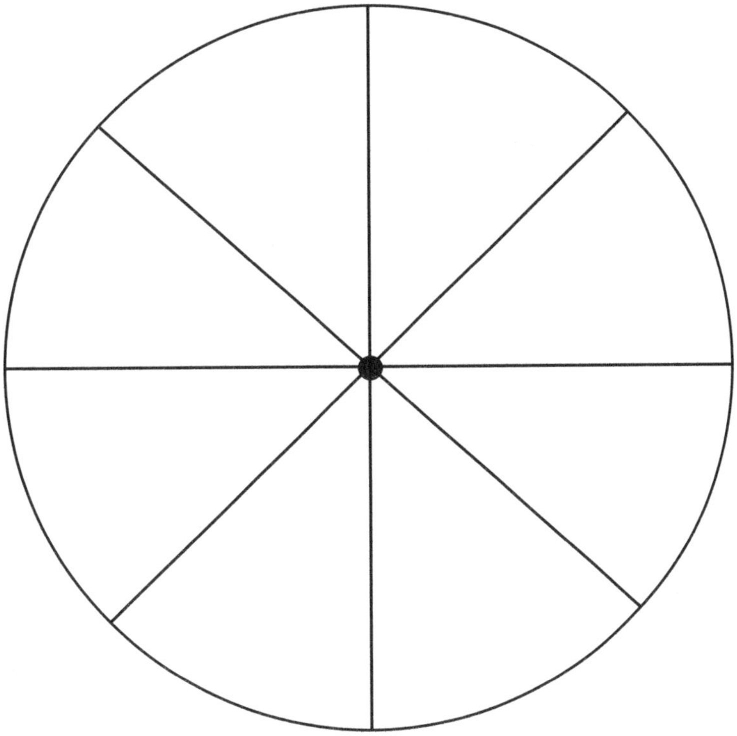

Resiliency Travel Kit

Purpose:

- Create a personalized "to-go," "go-to" travel kit for when boosts of resiliency are needed at a moment's notice.

What you will need:

NOTE These are just ideas for items that you may include in your resiliency travel kit. You may add, change, and adjust based on individual needs and preferences.

- Pencil/school box, shoe box, storage container, or other small-lidded box
- Mini bottle of water
- Plastic re-freezable ice cubes
- A non-inflated balloon
- Silly putty, slime, squishee, water beads, plush toy, or other squeezable item
- Smooth stones, glass stones, or other smooth, naturalistic item
- Small music player or sound machine
- Mini bottle scents such as vanilla, cinnamon, lavender, essential oils, etc.
- Pictures, notes, or items belonging to trusted loved ones
- Hard candies in soothing flavors
- Pictures of yoga poses, mantras, or self-holding and heart-holding positions
- Clay, beads, markers and paper, coloring books, journal, etc.

Adult Instructions:

1. Explain to the child/children that fuzzy and flooded moments can happen anytime and anywhere. Tell them we want to be prepared for these moments so we can get back to a place where we feel calm and in control quickly.

2. Ask the child/children if they have ever been on a vacation or long trip. Ask if they have seen a medical kit (band aids, antibacterial ointment, etc.) when they go in a vehicle. Discuss how these kits keep us prepared for moments when we may need some medical care.

3. Review the items described above with child/children. Refer to the description page to better understand the purpose and how to use each of these items.

4. Allow the child/children to choose 5+ items to place in their kit.

5. Practice how and when to use this kit with child/children.

6. If possible, keep track of how often they use it, specific items used, what works best, and what could be switched for other items to be tested.

NOTE In order to provide a stronger sense of pride and ownership in the kit, you may allow the child/children to decorate the box that will hold their items for soothing.

Confidence-Boosting, Strength & Resilience

This final section serves to strengthen resiliency and boost sense of self. Adapting and rebounding from adversity, treating challenges and disappointments as opportunities, and developing an unwavering belief in oneself, are some of the main attributes in overcoming trauma and living prosperously.

These activities focus on challenging negative self-talk, developing productive and affirming perceptions of self and of experiences, and practicing gratitude and positive thinking.

Included in this section are reflective exercises that focus on both internal and external sources of strength and encouragement. These activities are meant to serve as a catalyst for developing a positive mindset, grit, and a lifelong ability to bounce back from adversity.

BUILDING RESILIENCY IN CHILDREN

 # Chuffle Tree's Challenge

Purpose:

- Recognize how to shift perceptions and re-create narratives in order to maintain a sense of control, positivity, and strength.

What you will need:

- One copy of the *Apple Cycle Shift Narrative*
- One copy of the *Apple Cycle Shift* activity page

Adult Instructions:

1. Reflect on previous activities.
2. Explain that, today, you are going to read the tale of an apple tree. Explain that this apple tree is facing a challenge and that, together, you are going to come up with a way to help this apple tree find a solution to the challenge that it continues to face.
3. Discuss what a plant needs to thrive (water, sunlight, avoidance of destructive insects, etc.).
4. Read the *Apple Cycle Shift Narrative* to the child/children. Discuss the mindset of the apple tree and how this is not a helpful or beneficial way of thinking. Reflect on:
   a. how he is avoiding the things that will help him,
   b. how he is not acknowledging things that he could do to improve, and
   c. how he is blaming everything around him instead of shifting his perspective in order to stop this cycle of bad apples each season.
5. Discuss the cycle of apples on this apple tree and identify the factors that could be leading to its less-than-fruitful harvest.
6. Discuss how, sometimes, we get ourselves stuck in a cycle of bad thinking. Just like Chuffle Tree, this cycle leads to the same negative place. Explain how shifting our thoughts cycle can sometimes help to change the cycle and to help us to feel better.

7. Identify the negative cycle that Chuffle Tree was stuck in. Reflect on things like:
    a. not recognizing or reflecting on his actions to perpetuate the cycle, and
    b. blaming others instead of focusing on how to look within himself to produce better outcomes.

8. Use this as a springboard to discuss our own negative narratives and thinking patterns, as well as how we can shift this cycle in order to get the bounty we'd like to achieve.

Apple Cycle Shift Narrative

Sweet Cider Orchard is a lovely living space for an apple tree. Ask any of the apple trees there and they will tell you that Sweet Cider gives them everything they need to feel happy, safe, and to produce the best and most bountiful apple harvest in the nation!

Well, ask any apple tree, except for Chuffle Tree. Ever since he could bear fruit, Chuffle has produced nothing but duds. His apples tend to be small, brownish in color, and all around unappetizing. Even the worms don't want to eat his apples!

Why?

Chuffle Tree blames this cycle of bad harvests on everything and everyone around him.

He blames the sunlight, saying that it's too bright and hot. In fact, whenever he has the chance to catch some rays, he chooses to find shade and to avoid it altogether.

He also blames the rain, saying that when it falls, he puts an umbrella up because he doesn't want to get wet.

He even blames his apple tree neighbors, saying that they reap the benefits of not being as kind to him, since he allows all of the worms, bugs, and beetles to come nosh on his leaves and apples as they are growing.

If you ask him, Chuffle Tree does everything right to make the most tasty and vibrant apples around. He would say that each season, he does his best, but that each season, other factors come into play, forcing his apples to be, well… less than best.

"It just doesn't make sense," Chuffle Tree once said. "I do the same thing every season, and every season I get the same results. Dud apples."

How can we help Chuffle Tree to change this cycle for the next apple season?

NAME: _____   DATE: _____

Apple Cycle Shift Activity Page

Directions: Answer the below questions.

What advice would you give to this apple tree? How do you think it could change its way of thinking in order to grow a more healthy and bountiful harvest this coming apple season?

_____
_____
_____

What do you think the apple tree looks like now? Illustrate below.

What do you think the apple tree would look like if it took your advice? Illustrate below.

How could shifting thought cycles be helpful when you feel stuck in a bad situation? _____
_____
_____
_____
_____

Apple POP!

Purpose:
- Identify negative thoughts, experiences, or sources of unwelcome feelings.
- Release unwelcome feelings, thoughts, and emotions.

What you will need:
- Red, green, and yellow (apple colored) balloons
- Markers that can write on balloons

Adult Instructions:
1. Reflect on previous activities.
2. Discuss how we sometimes carry negative thoughts, feelings, and emotions with us that may be caused by one, or many, experiences. Discuss why this is not a good thing to carry.
3. Explain that, today, you will identify some of the negative experiences and unwelcome thoughts, feelings, or emotions that you may carry. Share that you will reflect on how big or small these things are, or how much they fill up our mind space, and will find a way to release them in order to allow for more positive thoughts to fill our mind space.
4. Hand the child/children 3-5 balloons. They may have more if needed.
5. Ask the child/children to reflect on an unwelcome experience or thought that has been filling their mind space. Tell them they have the choice to either share with you, or they may keep these reflections to themselves. If needed, provide examples of negative thoughts, feelings, emotions, or experiences.
6. Once the child/children have an idea in their heads, ask them to think about how much space this thing takes up in their mind. Does it take over their thoughts often? Is it just there sometimes but not too big? Is it the size of an apple seed or the size of a giant apple in their mind?
7. Ask the child/children to blow up one of the balloons to the size that they feel this is in their mind space (blow up just a little bit if it doesn't take up too much mind space, and so forth).
8. Tie the balloon for them as needed.

9. If they would like, they may use the marker to write or draw symbols to represent the unwelcome thought or experience on the corresponding balloon.

10. Continue doing this with the remaining balloons, or until they feel satisfied that they have identified all of their negative and unwelcome thoughts and experiences.

11. Reflect on the balloon sizes and the mind space they take up. Explain how these thoughts can quickly be blown into something greater and bigger than you'd like them to be.

12. Explain it is important to find ways to release these negative thoughts and to free up our mind space in order to allow in more positive, happy, productive, and overall better thoughts.

13. Using the previous activities as a starting point, brainstorm with the child/children ways they can release these negative thoughts in order to allow more positive ones to enter in.

14. Ask the child/children to pick up one of the balloons and identify at least one way they can release this negative thought. Once they have one in mind, allow them to squeeze or prick the balloon in order to pop it.

15. Continue doing so until each balloon is popped.

16. Reflect on the space these balloons take up now versus when they were full. Discuss thoughts that now have room to move in. Consider prompting with positive themes such as:
    a. ideas for self-care,
    b. goal setting and future-forward thoughts,
    c. points of gratitude,
    d. loving memories and images,
    e. jokes and laughable moments, and
    f. confidence boosters.

 One Bad Apple

Purpose:

- Identify negative thoughts, experiences, or sources of unwelcome feelings.
- Understand the impact of a negative thought.
- Determine ways to mitigate negative thoughts.

What you will need:

- One lidded box or container
- Squeezable paint
- A pack of ping pong balls, marbles, small apples, or other light and easy-to-find spherical medium

Adult Instructions:

1. Reflect on previous activities.
2. Tell the child/children you will be making an observation today through an artistic experiment.
3. Ask the child/children if they have ever heard the phrase, **"Don't let one bad apple spoil the whole bunch."**
4. Discuss the meaning of this phrase.
5. Reflect on the previous activity, *"Apple POP!"* Highlight the main understandings from this activity, including:
   a. how easily negative thoughts can blow up into something bigger than you'd like them to be,
   b. the amount of mind space negative thoughts can take up,
   c. the amount of mind space negative thoughts take away from positive thoughts, and
   d. how to POP negative thoughts in order to make room for more positive and productive thoughts.
6. Explain that, today, you will look at how one bad apple, or one negative thought, can impact the rest of the bunch.
7. Place all but one of the spherical items inside of the box.
8. Hand the remaining item to the child/children and instruct them to cover it in paint.

9. They may squeeze paint all over the item, on certain spots, or however they would like. Tell them to have fun!

10. Tell the child/children this paint represents rotting spots on a bad apple.

11. Once they have finished this task, ask them to give you a hypothesis:

    What do you think will happen when you place this item with these rotten spots inside of the container with the other items?

12. Discuss, then ask them to place the painted item in with the rest.

13. Discuss what you observe about the items directly hitting the painted one.

14. Place the lid on the container.

15. Ask the child/children for another hypothesis:

    What do you think will happen when we shake the box, allowing the "rotten apples" to touch the remaining ones?

16. Discuss.

17. Shake, shake, shake the box, as much as they would like.

18. When finished, open the lid and discuss what you observe.

19. Use this as a springboard to discuss the impact of one negative thought and how this could serve as a chain reaction, impacting other thoughts.

20. You could also use this as a time to discuss the alternative:

    How one POSITIVE thought can be used to spread good thoughts all around!

21. Conclude by sharing ways to:
    a. stop negative thoughts in their tracks, and to
    b. find ways to challenge and change negative thoughts.

NOTE

Ideas for how to challenge negative thoughts, and how to stop them in their tracks, can be found in the "Snap Skills" section of the *Building Resiliency in Youth* guide.

Apple Bird Feeder

Purpose:

- Practice the simple grounding technique of a mindful nature walk.
- Practice the act of doing good/helping.
- Reflect on the overall impact of these actions on self (mind, body, emotions).

What you will need:

- 1 apple
- Peanut butter (or another nut butter in case of allergies)
- Birdseed
- 1 spoon
- 1 bowl
- String
- A safe trail or path to take a nature walk on

Adult Instructions:

1. Explain that sometimes when we are feeling bad, doing things for others can make us feel good. Share stories of when you have helped someone or something. Discuss why being a helper might make us feel better.

   NOTE The child/children may be prompted by asking about a time when they have helped a friend, teacher, pet, the community, etc. You may also prompt with ideas such as holding the door for someone, picking a friend up who tripped, caring for a pet, helping to set the dinner table, cleaning, etc.

2. Explain how something as simple as being in nature and taking a walk outside can also make us feel better. Share and model ways to enhance the impact of nature on our well-being such as:

   a. paying attention to our senses (what do you see, hear, smell, feel),
   b. focusing on the present, being in the moment, and letting all other thoughts drift away with the breeze, or
   c. deep purposeful breathing and fully taking in the fresh air.

3. Tell the child/children that, today, you will participate in two acts: helping nature by providing birds and wildlife with nutrition, and taking a nature walk to practice the ways this can enhance well-being.

4. Cut the apple in half and tie the string either to the apple stem or pierce the apple and attach the string.

5. Pour birdseed into the bowl.

6. Explain to the child/children they may use the spoon to cover the apple in peanut butter (or another nut butter). You may want to ask they do this over the bowl of birdseed to avoid too much of a mess.

7. Ask the child/children to then dip and roll the nut butter-covered apple in the birdseed.

8. Take the child/children outside on a slow, calm, and peaceful nature walk. Be sure to remind them of the exercises discussed earlier to enhance the impact of the walk. Take the time to model and practice these exercises with them.

9. Allow the child/children to choose a tree or some other strong object from which they can hang the apple bird feeder from.

10. Once the feeder has been hanged, take a moment to soak in the moment. Remain as still and quiet as possible but guide the child/children with prompts:
    a. Ask them to close their eyes and to focus on what they hear (bird chirps, breeze through leaves, etc.) and feel (cool breeze, warm sun, etc.).
    b. Breathe in through your nose on a count of 3 and out slowly on a count of 4 (model and do with them).
    c. Look around and consider all of the creatures that they are providing food for (birds, squirrels, chipmunks, etc.).

11. Take a moment to reflect with the child/children. Ask them questions such as:
    a. How did our walk make you feel?
    b. How did providing food for these animals make you feel?
    c. How does it feel knowing you helped other living things today?
    d. Can you imagine times when helping others or taking a nature walk might help you if you are feeling down?
    e. Where could you safely walk at home, at school, around the community?
    f. What trusted adults could you walk with?
    g. What are some easy ways you could help other people or things?

Superstar Inside

Purpose:

- Recognize one's positive qualities and increase confidence.

What you will need:

- 2-3 apples, each from a different variety
- One paring knife
- *Superstar Inside* reflection page

Adult Instructions:

1. Explain to the child/children they will be enjoying a healthy snack today, but first you will be doing a little experiment.

2. Show the child/children the apples. Ask them to describe what they notice. What about them is similar? Different? What do they think each apple will taste like?

NOTE You may want to provide them with a verb word bank to draw ideas from (crisp, tart, sweet, juicy, grainy, mushy, bitter, etc.)

3. Tell the child/children that each of these apples comes from a different variety. That there are many apple varieties and that each variety has a star quality. Some may be very sweet and good for snacking, others may be tart and good for baking, while others still may be mushier and good for applesauce or cider. Explain that these apples come from different trees and different experiences. Ask the child/children if they can share any star qualities about their best friend, a family member, a teacher, etc. They may need help with words or with understanding what a "quality" is.

Example:

4. Ask the child/children if they know what is in the center of the apple. Discuss the apple core. Explain that the core holds the seeds and that these seeds share the same qualities of the apple. Tell them every apple has a core, and that the seeds inside the core can be planted to help more apple trees grow.

5. Tell the child/children you will be cutting the apples in half to see their cores.

6. Place the first apple on its side so that the stem and bottom are vertical, not horizontal.

7. Cut the first apple in half, making sure to cut with the stem and bottom facing vertically.

   Example:

8. Ask the child/children what shape the core and seeds make. Explain this apple may look plain but that it is a superstar inside. That the seeds hold the superstar qualities that can be used to spread more of these qualities in the world.

9. Ask them what they think will happen when you cut the next apple. Repeat this process until you have cut all the apples.

10. Share your observations. Explain that even though every apple had a different purpose and came from a different variety/experience, they all have a core and that each core shows they are all superstars inside.

11. Use this to start a discussion about the child/children and other children. Discuss how even though we all come from different places, different experiences, and have different purposes, we all have qualities that make us superstars inside. Also, use this time to discuss similarities. Just like apples, we all have a core that holds our superstar qualities like seeds. We can choose to let these qualities shine and can spread them to make the world a better place.

12. Complete the *Superstar Inside* reflection page.

NAME: _____   DATE:_____

Superstar Inside

Directions: Make obversations of the cut apples in the chart below.

My observations:

	Apple #1	Apple #2	Apple #3
Looks like			
Smells like			
Tastes like			

This is a picture of what I observed when we cut the apples in half.

Superstar Inside *(continued)*

We are all superstars in our cores.

Just like apple seeds, we can help the good qualities grow! My qualities make me a superstar, and I want to spread these qualities around to make the world a better place. I can do this by displaying my good qualities and work hard to let them grow!

Some of my good qualities are:

Pocket Apple Affirmations

Purpose:

- Reminder to maintain positivity, confidence, and strength.

What you will need:

- One old mint/candy tin, art matchbox (can be found online or in art stores), or other pocket-sized container
- Strips of paper to fit inside of the container
- Writing and coloring utensils
- Paint, glitter, and decorative materials

Adult Instructions:

1. Reflect on the previous activities, particularly *"Superstar Inside."*
2. Discuss confidence and self-love, the importance of recognizing one's own strengths, and the importance of remembering one's own strength and abilities even in times when one may feel applesauced.
3. Explain that, sometimes, we all need reminders of just how unique and amazing we are and how much of a superstar we are inside.
4. Tell the child/children that, today, we will be creating a little self-love reminder that we can always carry with us.
5. Give the child/children time to decorate the outside of the tin, art matchbox, or pocket-sized container.
6. Ask them to think of one word that makes them feel good and that instantly reminds them of how wonderful they are.

    NOTE This may be difficult for them. You may prompt them with examples or ideas such as "joker," "artist," "sports star," "poet," "friend," "caterer," "chef," "strong person," etc.

7. Using paint or marker, write that word on the inside of the container.
8. Next, discuss the positive traits, skills, and things that make each child unique and amazing.

    NOTE You may come up with your own, ask the group if this is in a group setting, or ask them what they think friends would say are wonderful skills and qualities that each child holds.

9. Write these things on each strip of paper. Then fold and place inside the container.

10. Tell the child/children they can carry this with them wherever they go, or keep it in a safe place.

11. Explain that in those moments when they need a little reminder of what makes them a superstar inside (as we all sometimes do), they can simply open this container and read these words.

 Seeds of Gratitude

Purpose:

- Illustrate the importance of gratitude.
- Identify people, places, and/or things one is grateful for.

What you will need:

- 1 plastic baggie
- 1 damp paper towel
- Seeds from 1-3 apples
- *Seeds of Gratitude* worksheet

Adult Instructions:

1. Discuss the term "gratitude" with the child/children.
2. Explain how even in the worst of times or even when we have stinky or unwelcome feelings, there is always something to be grateful for.
3. Brainstorm a list of things to be grateful for. If necessary, prompt with labels such as people/places/things.
4. Explain how: (a) realizing the little things to be grateful for, and (b) practicing gratitude every day, allows us to (c) feel more confident, (d) let unwelcome or unhappy experiences melt away quicker, and (e) feel happier overall.
5. Discuss the small ways to practice gratitude everyday (take a moment each morning to think of one thing they are grateful for to start the day and a moment at night to think of one thing they are grateful for from the day, make a list of things they are grateful for and keep it close by, do something kind for someone, etc.).
6. Explain how, much like a tiny appleseed can grow into a magnificent fruitful tree, when you recognize the small seeds of good, plant them, and give them time to grow, you provide yourself with the elements needed to grow a strong and positive mindset. This makes you feel happier overall, and you spread that happiness to those around you.
7. Tell the child/children you will be doing two things today: an experiment and another activity.
8. Show the child/children the plastic baggie and dampened paper towel. Ask them to fold the towel into halves or fourths (depending on the size of the bag) and carefully place the towel inside of the bag, trying to be sure the towel covers the inside of the bag.

9. Allow the child/children to carefully place the seeds in the bag and on various spaces in the folded towel.

10. Place the towel in a cool, but sunlit area.

11. Tell the child/children you will practice control and patience by allowing the seeds time and by coming back to check on the seeds every week or so for the next few weeks.

    NOTE While the majority of seeds may not produce much movement, some will sprout and begin to show light green leaves. This will not grow into a tree, but it is still fun to observe!

12. Complete the *Seeds of Gratitude* worksheet.

NAME: _____ DATE: _____

Seeds of Gratitude

Directions: In each seed, write or draw something (person, place, thing) that you are grateful for.

A Trauma-Informed Activity Guide for Children

 Picking & Choosing Joy

Purpose:

- Promote reflection of the lighter things/maintaining a positive outlook.
- Practice shifting focus to maintain a more positive outlook.

What you will need:

- One copy of the *Picking & Choosing Joy* worksheet

Adult Instructions:

1. Reflect on the previous activities.
2. Remind the child/children that, even though it is hard sometimes, there is always something to be grateful for and something to find the light in. Discuss how changing your outlook and searching for the positives helps us to overcome challenges, become stronger, maintain control, and encourage overall wellness.
3. Complete the *Picking & Choosing Joy* worksheet with the child/children. They may choose to draw or write in the things that bring them joy.
4. If possible, explore online or in books to find jokes, silly and/or comforting images that evoke joy, favorite TV shows or games, etc.
5. When finished, discuss the various things that the child/children included in their tree. Remind them they can look back and remember these things in times of need.

NAME: _____   DATE: _____

Picking & Choosing Joy

Directions: Think of the things that bring you joy. This can be people, places, things, games, characters, funny jokes, anything you'd like. Write or draw them in the apples below. Use this as a reminder that in moments of unwelcome feelings, you can pick one of these apple items and you can choose joy.

© 2021, Father Flanagan's Boys' Home

Apple Up!

Purpose:
- Identify strategies to promote overall wellness following undesired experiences.
- Reflect on how these strategies can translate into real life.

What you will need:
- One set of *"I'm feeling…"* cards
- One set of *Apple Superhero* cards
- One set of *Apple Up!* cards
- One set of *Apple Cutouts*

Adult Instructions:

1. Prepare beforehand by cutting out the *"I'm feeling…"* cards, the *Apple Superhero* cards, *Apple Up!* cards, and the *Apple Cutouts*.
2. Place the sets of cards in two piles (one pile of *"I'm feeling…"* cards, one pile of *Apple Superhero* cards).
3. Place the *Apple Cutouts* into one pile.
4. Provide each player with three *Apple Up!* cards.
5. To play:
   a. Explain the superpowers and traits of each Apple Superhero to the child/children. Use this as a discussion point to reflect on what they have learned so far about each superpower.
   b. Choose who will go first.
   c. Player one will pick up an *"I'm feeling…"* card and read aloud, as well as the amount of apple cutouts earned for providing a superhero action (you may choose to read for the child, if needed).
   d. Player one will then choose one of the *Apple Superhero* cards and read the superpower connected to that Apple Superhero.

BUILDING RESILIENCY IN CHILDREN

e. In order to earn the identified amount of apple cutouts, the player must provide one strategy, or superhero action, to help alleviate the scenario. The superhero action they share must align with the Apple Superhero's superpower written on the card they chose.

f. Player two then goes.

g. If the player on deck cannot think of a superhero action, the other player may have a chance to pick that player's apples by throwing one "Apple Up" card down and sharing a superhero action.

h. Take turns picking cards and providing superhero actions until all cards are finished.

i. The player with the most apple cutouts at the end gets to choose the conclusion of the session (turn on music and dance, yoga, tell jokes, play another game, create art, etc.).

A Trauma-Informed Activity Guide for Children

Apple Superhero Cards

CARD FRONTS

NOTE: *All of the cards and card-backs are available as a download for double-sided print.*

Apple Superhero Cards

CARD FRONTS

Apple Superhero Cards

CARD BACKS

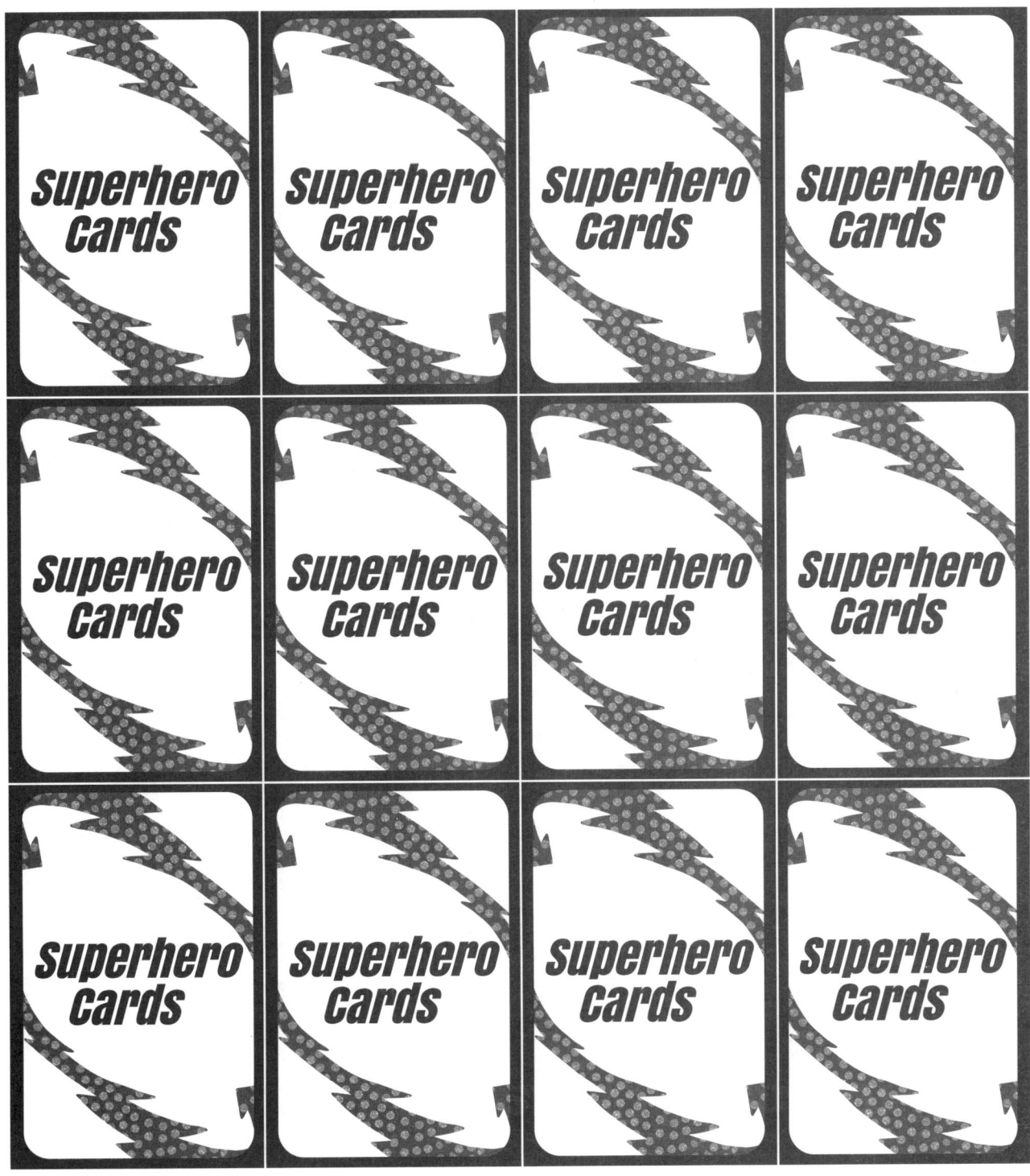

"I'm feeling…" Cards

CARD FRONTS

RIGHT NOW, I'm feeling really scared. I need a superhero action to help me calm down…

RIGHT NOW, I feel like crying and need a superhero action to help me calm down…

RIGHT NOW, I'm feeling really unhappy and need a superhero action to help me calm down…

RIGHT NOW, I'm feeling really ashamed and need a superhero action to help me calm down…

RIGHT NOW, I'm feeling really angry and need a superhero action to help me calm down…

RIGHT NOW, I'm feeling really confused and need a superhero action to help me calm down…

RIGHT NOW, I'm feeling really sad and need a superhero action to help me calm down…

RIGHT NOW, I'm feeling worried and need a superhero action to help me calm down…

RIGHT NOW, I'm feeling really afraid and need a superhero action to help me calm down…

RIGHT NOW, I'm feeling really mad and need a superhero action to help me calm down…

RIGHT NOW, I'm feeling really worthless and need a superhero action to help me calm down…

RIGHT NOW, I'm feeling really unloved and need a superhero action to help me calm down…

"I'm feeling..." Cards

CARD FRONTS

RIGHT NOW, I'm feeling really scared. I need a superhero action to help me calm down...

RIGHT NOW, I feel like crying and need a superhero action to help me calm down...

RIGHT NOW, I'm feeling really unhappy and need a superhero action to help me calm down...

RIGHT NOW, I'm feeling really ashamed and need a superhero action to help me calm down...

DRAW YOUR OWN

DRAW YOUR OWN

DRAW YOUR OWN

DRAW YOUR OWN

DRAW YOUR OWN

DRAW YOUR OWN

DRAW YOUR OWN

DRAW YOUR OWN

"I'm feeling..." Cards

CARD BACKS

Apple Up! Cards

NOTE *Front and backs of cards are provided for download and print.*

Apple Cutouts

A Trauma-Informed Activity Guide for Children

 The Big Apple

Purpose:

- Identify personal strengths.
- Gain confidence in self and increase self-love.
- Celebrate the completion of this workbook.

What you will need:

- Party materials (crafts, games, treats, etc.)
- One copy of *What Makes You the Big Apple*

Adult Instructions:

1. Use this time to celebrate the culmination of these activities. Share stories, reflect on new learnings, and discuss how to carry these new learnings into the future.

2. During the celebration, acknowledge all of the hard work that the child/children have demonstrated. Praise, have fun, and enjoy some laughs.

3. Complete and gift the youth with *What Makes You the Big Apple*.

NAME: _____ DATE: _____

What Makes You the Big Apple

In an orchard of apples, you are the brightest, shiniest, most vibrant superstar apple.

YOU are the BIG APPLE.
I think this because…

I have loved our time together. **Keep on shining!**

Best,

_____

Children's Read-Aloud

The following story is designed to accompany the activities in this guide. The stories and illustrated pages are available for download, and the art is designed as coloring pages.

See instructions for downloading the story included in the Table of Contents.

Dear parent, teacher, or caregiver,

Below are useful prompts and guidance for making the most of this read-aloud.

First, there are two introductions provided. One is geared toward upper elementary-aged children, and the second is geared toward younger children. Use the introduction that best suits your needs.

Secondly, below are some recommended book prompts to further engage children in discussion and learning around the content of this story.

Feelings and Frustrations at Sweet Cider Orchard
Children's Read-Aloud Book Prompts

PAGE 5

1. As orchard elder, Granny Smith takes care of all of the apples of Sweet Cider Orchard and wants to ensure that they are all happy to the core. Who is the Granny Smith in your life? Who are the people who care for you and want you to feel happy to the core?

PAGE 5

2. Granny Smith noticed that some of the apples had been feeling rotten. How can you tell when other people aren't feeling very happy? How can people tell when you aren't feeling happy?

PAGE 5

3. Granny Smith says that seeing the apples in her orchard feeling unhappy makes her feel "applesauced." What do you think she means by that?

PAGE 5

4. Granny Smith mentions that trusting each other, sharing feelings, and supporting one another is brave. Why do you think it takes bravery to share feelings and to support one another?

PAGE 7

5. Jazz explains that letting others know how you feel is like planting seeds. That when you allow others to nurture and care for you, it gives you the strength to grow happier and healthier. What do you think he means by this? Have you ever planted a seed like this? Who are some trusted people that you could share your feelings with?

PAGE 9

6. What do you think Golden Delicious meant when he said "Just because she looks crisp and fresh on the outside doesn't mean that she isn't bruised inside…" about Gala?

PAGE 9

7. Do you think acting this way makes Gala feel better? Do you think this is the best way to solve problems? What do you think Gala could do instead of always trying to be the life of the party?

PAGE 9

8. When Gala said, "Thank you for listening. I feel better already, just knowing that I am not carrying this heavy load alone," what do you think she meant?

PAGE 11

9. Golden Delicious talks about looking fancy, prim, proper, and polished to others but, inside, he doesn't feel that way at all. Why do you think he hides the truth? Have you ever felt like you had to hide your feelings around others?

PAGE 15

10. Even though their experiences were very different, Jazz and Fuji both felt alone. Like they were oddballs out. Have you ever felt like you didn't belong? Have you ever felt something that a peer has felt, even though you had different experiences that caused these feelings?

PAGE 17

11. When McIntosh said, "I want to be invisible," what do you think she meant? If you were her friend, what would you say to her? How would you help her overcome the bullying?

PAGE 17

12. Jona Rotten has a reputation for being a bad apple. Why does he act this way? Is he really a bad and mean apple? Have you ever met someone who acts like Jona Rotten? What are some reasons that people may act unkindly? What could you do to help?

PAGE 19

13. Granny Smith points out the fact that, after sharing out, everyone knows what is going on inside themselves and inside of each other. Why is it important to know what you are feeling? Why is it important to know what others are feeling?

PAGE 20

14. Which "feel better" strategies have you tried? Have any of these helped you to feel better? Which ones do you think you would like to try? Can you think of other "feel better" strategies that Granny Smith could write on the barn wall?

PAGE 22

15. Which "problem-solving" strategies have you tried? Have any of these helped solve problems that you have had? Which ones do you think you would like to try? Can you think of other "problem-solving" strategies that the apples could write on the barn wall?

PAGE 23

16. Why do you think checking in with each other, paying attention to each other's feelings, and giving each other support was important?

Introduction for UPPER elementary ages

Feelings and Frustrations at Sweet Cider Orchard

PAGE 5

The sound of rustling autumn leaves filled the air as the moon lit up the wooden barn. It was a crisp evening at Sweet Cider Orchard. All of the apples rolled off of their trees and bobbled into the barn, curiously whispering to each other in anticipation of the night's discussion.

Cortland stood at the entrance, handing out mugs of her famous spiced cider to everyone as they passed.

"Thank you, Cortland!" Jazz apple exclaimed with a twirl. "I wonder why Granny Smith called for an orchard harvest meeting. She must have something important to talk about!"

"You're right about that, Jazz," Cortland responded. "Granny Smith only calls for orchard harvest meetings when there is something as pressing as cider to share!"

Jazz nodded his head in agreement as Granny Smith slowly and proudly entered the barn. Every apple in the orchard grew silent as she carefully took her spot on a large bale of hay where every orchard apple could see her.

"Welcome, friends. I appreciate you coming out tonight. I have something very important that I would like to discuss with you all. Something that has been troubling me lately. Something that makes me feel grainy inside. My hope is that we can talk about it and work together to fix it."

All of the apples stood motionless, watching the honorable Granny Smith as she looked down to the dirt floor and took in a deep breath. After a moment, she looked back at her orchard companions, and began again.

"As orchard elder, it is my responsibility to guide you and ensure you always feel sweetness and joy. You are all the apples of my eye. However, lately I've noticed that many of you seem to be feeling a little rotten. Some of you seem sad and just plain *applesauced,* some of you seem angry and fit to be pied, while others seem like your stems are about to pop at any moment! I was hoping that we could have a brave talk tonight. We can share what we have been feeling, why we have felt this way, and we can work together to help make this orchard *a-ppleasing* and *apple-ayful* place for everyone."

"Phewy!" Crabapple exclaimed with a sour scowl. "What's good is it going to do to talk about these things?"

"Having a safe and trusted core friend or bushel of friends to share your experiences with is always helpful," Granny Smith said. "They make you feel like you are not alone, and they can offer support like a warm hug and a kind word! They can also help you think of ways to feel better... ways that you may not have thought of before! If you are able to recognize and share your feelings and what caused them, you can better understand how to help yourself feel better when those feelings sprout up again."

© 2021, Father Flanagan's Boys' Home

Introduction for YOUNGER ages

Feelings and Frustrations at Sweet Cider Orchard

PAGE 7

It was a cool autumn night at Sweet Cider Orchard. All of the apples gathered into the barn, where Granny Smith waited.

Cortland handed out mugs of her famous warm-spiced cider as Granny Smith climbed onto the basket podium to speak.

"Hello, friends!" Granny Smith said kindly and smiled. "Thank you for joining us tonight. We have a bushel of things to talk about!

"As orchard elder here at Sweet Cider Orchard, I want to be sure that each and every one of you feels happy to the core. Which is why I called for this apple gathering.

"I have noticed that some of you seem to be feeling a little rotten lately, and that makes me feel *apple-sauced*. I was hoping we could talk about it! That we could trust each other enough to share the things that have been eating at us, and that we could be brave enough to offer support for each other. After all, I want our little orchard to be *ap-playful* and *ap-pleasing* for one and all!"

"Oh, phewy!" Crabapple scowled. "I don't need to talk to anyone about anything! This makes me fit to be pied! Hmph, what good can talking do?"

"Well, you have seemed a little crabbier than normal, Crabapple." Jazz sang out with pizzazz. "I'll bet that letting others know how you are feeling is like planting seeds. Instead of letting these feelings seeds scatter and blow out of control, you keep them in one safe place where others can nurture them with their ideas and care. That then gives you the strength to sprout up and grow happier and healthier than before!"

"Phewy! Not a chance!" Crabapple huffed as he rolled onto a hay bale.

"None of you would understand anyway. No, thank you! I will just sit right here and watch you all waste your time with this," Crabapple snarled.

Granny Smith slowly crept over to Crabapple and gently touched his stem with hers, "That's okay, Crabapple. You do not have to share unless you want to. We appreciate your company either way. And who knows, maybe you can help one of your fellow apples! The offer to share is always here. I know it's scary or may seem pointless at first but I do hope you will."

"Hmph!" Crabapple sneered.

Story after introduction(s)

Gala sprouted up and cheered. **"Can I go first? I have something that needs to be said."**

The other apples looked at Gala, then at each other in confusion.

"You, Gala? You have something to say?" McIntosh asked, puzzled. "But, you're always so upbeat and the life of the party! How can you have something bothering you?"

"Just because she looks crisp and fresh on the outside doesn't mean she isn't bruised inside," Golden Delicious said gently from the back of the barn. "Trust me, I know. Just let her share."

Gala continued, "It's true. I'm the first to crack a joke. I'm the one you turn to when you want a laugh or to be entertained. I am adventurous and daring. I am always the life of the party and act like I don't have a care in the world. The fact is though, I only do this because I don't want to feel what is really inside. Sadness, emptiness, and fear. You see, my tree was hit by lightning last year, splitting it in half. I was just a little bud at the time but many of my budding siblings that were growing on the branches fell away from me. I have not seen them since. I don't know where they are, and I miss them. That experience, and not knowing what happened to my loved ones, has left me shaken to the core. I don't want to think about it, or feel the way I feel, so I pretend. I make others laugh to try and forget about my pain. I act silly and crazy because I don't know what else to do. I just want to be louder than the unwelcome feelings inside."

"Oh, Gala." Cortland sighed. "I had no idea. I wish I knew what I could say to make things better."

"Thank you for listening. I feel better already, just knowing that I am not carrying this heavy load alone." Gala grinned and shuffled her leaves.

Gala asked, "Golden Delicious, how about you? It sounds like you might understand what it's like to put on an *a-peeling* coat and pretend like you are happy when deep inside you feel grainy. If you want to talk about it, we are all here to listen."

Golden Delicious took a big gulp of cider before nervously speaking. "I... I... I don't really know where to start. I guess, well... you all know who I am. I'm part of the Golden family. We have the fanciest tree in the orchard, we ride in the most modern tractors, and we always look prim and polished whenever we strut around the orchard. You probably think we set like strudel. The thing is, though, it's not that easy.

"You see, my parents have been fighting a lot lately. Sometimes it's really bad. They say mean things to each other, and to me. They are so loud that it makes me unable to sleep at night. On top of that, they are both so busy harvesting long hours or fighting with each other that they even forget to give me sunlight and nutrients. They always tell me that I'm not shiny enough, or that I'm too mealy. I feel like I will never be the apple they want me to be. I have been feeling sad, ashamed, guilty, scared, and nervous."

"Wow. I would have never known that, Golden Delicious," Granny Smith empathized. "I guess I have noticed that you are more quiet than normal and less enthusiastic about playing with the other apples lately."

Jazz trumpeted, "I guess a lot of us are putting on a vibrant face for the orchard, but when you look past the polished peel, we are *applesauced* inside. **Thank you for sharing this, Golden Delicious. I know what it's like to hide and feel ashamed and scared. I am here for you.**"

Feelings and Frustrations at Sweet Cider Orchard

"Thank you, Jazz! Maybe you can tell us what you mean when you say you are putting on a vibrant face? I'd like to see if I can help you, too."

Jazz twirled and giggled, unsure of what to say.

"Gosh. It's been going on for so long that I almost don't feel it anymore! It's almost like I don't care what anyone says about me but... here it goes....

"I feel so alone. Like an orange in an apple's body. You see, all of the other apple boys in the orchard have different tastes than me. They like to talk about the farm equipment and play apple toss. I tried to like those things, too. But, I don't. Instead of farm equipment, I like to talk about the latest trends in harvest colors. Instead of apple toss, I'd much rather dance the Apple Dapple. I like to sing and dance and all that pizzazz, even though I know the others don't. As hard as I try, I just can't fit in. It almost feels like there is something wrong with me and that I should be ashamed of who I am.

What adds even more crumble to the top of that cake is the way others treat me. Just because I like different things, just because I look and sound different, they make fun of me. They call me names, say that I have 'mealworm cooties' and refuse to get near me, and they even threaten to smash me into apple butter. They do it all the time. I'm so scared, confused, and alone. It's been happening for so long though that I've gotten used to it. In fact, I'm even starting to believe some of the mean things they call me. I guess there is something wrong with me." Jazz lowered his head and wilted.

All of the apples sat in silence, mulling over Jazz's words. Many of them looking back and realizing just how intolerant they have been to Jazz: excluding him from orchard events, laughing when others made fun of him, ignoring him, or not standing up for him when others were unkind to him.

Feelings and Frustrations at Sweet Cider Orchard

Before anyone could respond, Fuji chimed in.

"An orange in an apple's body? Gosh. I know what you mean. I feel like I'm an apple in a grove of oranges! Ever since we were forced to move here after my old orchard was attacked by an infestation of beetles, I've felt so out of place. I lost all of my belongings, my friends, and my home. Suddenly uprooted and thrown into this new place where everything is different. Everyone in Sweet Cider Orchard looks different, talks different, and acts different. It's hard enough losing everything I knew so suddenly but trying to keep up with this new life makes it even harder.

"Sometimes I can't tell if I'm sad, mad, scared, up, down, left, right... everything is so confusing. I feel like I'm spinning and have no control over how fast or how long I go. I have a lot of bad nightmares and am always thinking about the night we had to leave. It makes me explode with anger sometimes. I feel like I can't stop myself and that I'm always waiting for the next unexpected scary thing to happen."

"May I say something?" McIntosh asked. "Um, I know you all think of me as the intellectual. I'm the orchard bookworm, always planted in a book, studying, learning... but, like Gala, this is sort of my way of avoiding unwelcome feelings. Instead of being the life of the party, I'm the quiet shadow that hides behind my studies. I want to be invisible. The reason for this is the Rotten Apple Gang. You know, the family of bad apples that goes around the orchard ripping stems and leaves, cracking branches...." McIntosh took a deep breath and began again. "They have been targeting me with their bullying ways, especially Jona Rotten."

"WHAT DO YOU KNOW, McINTOSH?" Jona Rotten snapped. "YOU THINK EVERYTHING IN MY LIFE IS ALL JONAGOLD AND HONEYCRISP?" He suddenly felt the warmth of Granny Smith's touch, causing him to simmer down.

"Sorry. It's just, things are tough for me, okay? And if things are tough for me, I need to act toughER towards everyone else. It's the only way to feel better, even though it never actually does make me feel better."

"Please, Jona. Tell us what is tough for you. We want to help." McIntosh adjusted her glasses and gazed at Jona with sincerity.

Jona took a deep breath. "It's just... whenever I go home, I get the Rotten family treatment. My parents yell at me, throw stems and twigs so hard that I get bruised, and they tell me that I will never be Rotten enough. I have no choice but to be as rotten as I can to carry on the Rotten apple name. It's not like I WANT to be mean or hurtful... I HAVE to be. Otherwise, I will get it even worse from my family. Besides, I keep hoping that if I can make someone else feel as rotten as I do, I won't feel as bad."

"Does it make you feel better, Jona? Being mean to us?" McIntosh quivered, afraid to hear his answer.

"It only makes me feel even more sour and wormy inside."

Feelings and Frustrations at Sweet Cider Orchard

At that moment, Crabapple stood up. "It does make you feel more sour, and wormy, and just plain crabby to act like a bad apple, doesn't it? I know what you mean, Jona. I just wish I knew how to stop it, too. Once you start, it's like a tree sprouting up… you just can't stop it. No matter how hard you try."

For a moment. The orchard was silent. No one knew what to say. All they could do was stew in their thoughts. This was the first time they had realized the pain and hurt that the other apples were going through. The first time they understood the struggles of their orchard neighbors, and the first time they could connect to each other in that way.

"Well, my my my. I think we can all agree that we learned a lot today. About ourselves, about each other… maybe we even were able to find similarities that we didn't see before within each other." Granny Smith's stem straightened tall as she made her way to the podium.

"So, now that we understand what is really going on inside ourselves and our orchard friends, what can we do? How do we return to our old bright, sweet, and jolly ways? How can we help each other?"

Everyone took a moment, looking at each other, then back at Granny Smith.

"Maybe we can start by sharing things we do to make us feel better? Who knows? Maybe we will give each other new ideas or come up with a brand-new idea altogether, just by sharing!" Jazz squealed joyfully.

"Great idea, Jazz!" Granny Smith smiled. "I will get some chalk. You can take turns shouting out your ideas, and I will write them on our barn wall so that we can always refer back to them!"

With that, Granny Smith pulled out a piece of chalk and began writing, writing, and writing. Ideas were coming in faster than she could write! By the time the ideas had simmered like apple crisp, she had a wall full of **"feel better"** strategies.

CLOSE YOUR EYES, TAKE 3 DEEP BREATHS IN LIKE YOU'RE SNIFFING APPLE PIE, AND BREATHE OUT ALL OF THE BAD FEELINGS WITH EACH LONG EXHALE.

BREATHE IN DEEP, PICTURING WHAT YOU WANT TO FEEL LIKE AS YOU INHALE. BREATHE OUT, PICTURING WHAT YOU DON'T WANT TO FEEL GETTING BLOWN AWAY WITH EACH EXHALE.

TELL YOURSELF THAT YOU ARE OKAY. YOU ARE STRONG. YOU WILL GET THROUGH THIS. YOU DESERVE HAPPINESS.

GO FOR A STROLL OUTSIDE. LET YOUR MIND WANDER WITH YOU, FOCUSING ON THE SIGHTS, SOUNDS, SMELLS, AND FEELS.

DRAW THE THING THAT MAKES YOU FEEL BAD AS A MONSTER. THEN, DRAW YOURSELF DEFEATING THAT MONSTER WITH YOUR MIND STRENGTH.

DRAW THINGS THAT MAKE YOU HAPPY.

WRITE A LETTER TO SOMEONE WHO MAKES YOU HAPPY.

WRITE A LETTER TO YOURSELF ABOUT WHAT YOU FEEL, WHY, AND WHAT WOULD MAKE YOU FEEL BETTER.

BAKE WITH AN ADULT.

DANCE AND SING ALONG TO YOUR FAVORITE UPBEAT SONGS.

MAKE A CRAFT OR PERFORM A SCIENCE EXPERIMENT.

TAKE A WARM BATH OR RUN YOUR HANDS UNDER WARM WATER.

TOUCH WATER BEADS, SLIME, OR SHAVING CREAM.

PLAY WITH A PET.

DO SOMETHING NICE FOR SOMEONE.

PLAY OUTSIDE.

LISTEN TO, READ, OR WATCH THINGS THAT MAKE YOU LAUGH.

THINK ABOUT ALL OF THE PEOPLE, PLACES, AND THINGS THAT YOU ARE THANKFUL FOR.

DAYDREAM ABOUT SPACE AND OCEANS AND MAGIC AND THINGS THAT MAKE YOU HAPPY.

BLOW BUBBLES.

PRETEND YOUR BODY IS PIE DOUGH! SLOWLY STRETCH IT AND BEND IT IN WAYS THAT FEEL GOOD.

TALK TO A FRIEND OR AN ADULT THAT YOU TRUST.

"These are some wonderful ideas!" Crabapple beamed. "I would have never thought of many of them! Thank you for sharing!"

"They are wonderful, aren't they?" Granny Smith stepped back and admired all of the ideas. "BUT, we aren't finished! We have a good list of things to do to feel better, but they don't really solve the problems, do they?"

The orchard apples shook their heads in agreement.

"We know how to make ourselves feel better. Now, we need to figure out how to mend broken fences once we are feeling well enough to solve problems!" Gala exclaimed. "After all, if we don't find solutions to the things that bother us, they will just keep on eating away at us like inchworms!

"RIGHT!" The orchard apples all shouted in agreement. They may be apples, but the orchard neighbors paired up to talk about possible solutions to everyone's problems. Each pair of apples then wrote their ideas on another barn wall. What they came up with was amazing.

RESPOND WITH CONFIDENCE AND KINDNESS.

TALK TO SOMEONE YOU TRUST AND FEEL SAFE SHARING THINGS WITH.

AVOID LETTING OTHER PEOPLE CONTROL YOUR EMOTIONS.

STAY STRONG AND STICK TO WHAT YOU KNOW IS THE RIGHT AND GOOD THING TO DO.

STAY TRUE TO YOURSELF AND AVOID PEOPLE WHO MAKE YOU FEEL BAD.

ONLY KEEP FRIENDSHIPS WITH PEOPLE WHO SEE YOUR AWESOMENESS AND WANT TO BOOST YOU UP/HELP YOU FEEL GOOD.

IGNORE AND AVOID PEOPLE WHO MAKE YOU FEEL BAD ABOUT YOURSELF. THEY DON'T DESERVE YOUR TIME, EFFORT, OR ATTENTION.

DON'T BE AFRAID TO ASK FOR HELP FROM AN ADULT YOU TRUST AND FEEL SAFE WITH. YOU ARE NOT ALONE. YOU HAVE PEOPLE WHO WANT TO KEEP YOU SAFE AND HAPPY. TRUST THEM.

© 2021, Father Flanagan's Boys' Home

That night, all of the apples in Sweet Apple Orchard walked away with a little more pep in their steps. Knowing that they were not alone in their feelings and that others had similar feelings or similar stories, that they were able to share without being judged, and that they had each other for support gave them all a boost of fresh confidence and feelings that everything was going to be okay.

In the coming weeks, the apples checked in with each other. They made sure to pay attention to how each friend was feeling and to offer support. **Before long, Sweet Cider Orchard was once again a jolly, ap-playful, and ap-pleasing place to be.**

And they lived *apple-y* ever after.

References

Hannigan, S., Grima-Farrell, C., & Wardman, N. (2019). Drawing on creative arts therapy approaches to enhance inclusive school cultures and student wellbeing. *Issues in Educational Research, 29,* 756.

Malchiodi, C. A. (2018). *The Handbook of Art Therapy and Digital Technology.* Jessica Kingsley Publishers.

McGrady, K. (2021). *Building Resiliency in Youth: A Trauma-informed Guide for Working with Youth in Schools.* Omaha, NE: Boys Town Press.

Waite, R., & Ryan, R. A. (2019). *Adverse Childhood Experiences: What Students and Health Professionals Need to Know* (1st ed.). Routledge.